COLIN VOGEL

THE
HORSE'S
HEALTH
BIBLE

THE QUICK-REFERENCE GUIDE
TO THE DIAGNOSIS OF COMMON
VETERINARY PROBLEMS

David and Charles

A DAVID & CHARLES BOOK
David & Charles is a subsidiary of F+W (UK) Ltd.,
an F+W Publications Inc. company

First published in the UK in 2002
Reprinted 2002, 2003, 2004
First paperback edition 2005

Copyright © Colin Vogel 2002, 2005

Distributed in North America
by F+W Publications, Inc.
4700 E. Galbraith Rd.
Cincinnati, OH 45236
1-800-289-0963

A catalogue record for this book is available from the
British Library.

ISBN 0 7153 1285 5 hardback
ISBN 0 7153 2147 1 paperback

Jacket photos: Peter Gray (top right, 2nd from top
right, bottom right and 2nd from bottom left); all
others Kit Houghton

Commissioning Editor: Jane Trollope
Art Editor: Sue Cleave
Desk Editor: Tom McCann
Copy Editor: Anne Plume
Production Controller: Adrian Buckley

Printed in Singapore by KHL Printing Co Pte Ltd
for David & Charles
Brunel House Newton Abbot Devon

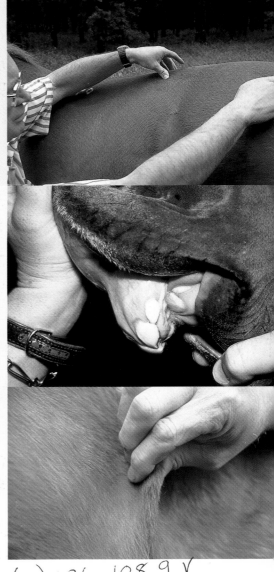

CONTENTS

How to Use this Book

This practical guide to interpreting your horse's symptoms, and dealing confidently with health problems, is divided into three easy-to-use sections. In order to help you make the most of this book, the role of each part is explained below. You will also find that just 'dipping in' will provide valuable information to help you maintain and improve your horse's wellbeing.

1 Flow Charts

In Part 1 there are 26 flow charts, each one presenting the likely interpretations of the symptoms indicated in its title. For example, for the question 'Why has my horse developed bald areas on its skin?': the flow chart indicates sweet itch; ringworm; mud fever, etc. The circled numbers next to the diagnoses refer to Part 2, where you can find more information concerning particular topics. Any bracketed page numbers after a diagnosis or symptom refer to Part 3.

75 Sweet itch

Ridges of thick skin along the neck and withers of a horse suffering from sweet itch

What is it? Sweet itch is an allergic disease. The horse injected into the skin by the Culicoides biting the horse rub the areas bitten by the mi is rubbed off and the skin rubbed **plasma/serum**). This disease occurs in th but it will take months for the hair to regr

How is it treated? Although benzyl benzoate applied to the a deterrent, treatment really depends on preve the use of insect repellents, this involves that the midges are most active (the first a cases the horse has to be stabled with a fi Once the symptoms occur only **steroids** irritation, and their use has to be undertak ger off laminitis, especially in ponies. Once to suffer from it in succeeding years, usually

76 Lice

What are they? There are two types of lice: biting lice and s cally the same, namely irritation that cause will be rubbed away and the skin may be n 120 are probably the worst affected.

2 Diagnoses

In Part 2, the diagnoses indicated just by name on the flow charts in Part 1 are explained. The entries in this section answer such questions as 'What is this disease/injury?', 'What is the treatment?' and 'How can it be avoided?'. Where possible associated symptoms and diagnoses are grouped together, so that, for example, all the possible causes of a horse's foot lameness can be found in the same place for easy reference. Within these entries words in bold type refer to an entry in Part 3, where many subjects are explained more fully.

3 Technical Terms Explained

Part 3 contains explanations of more technical procedures, some treatments that readers can perform themselves (several with step-by-step photographs), and technical terms such as 'ultrasound' and 'endotoxins'. For quick reference there is an alphabetical listing of all the entries in this section on page 134–5.

Identifying bald areas

Regular inspection of the horse's skin, particularly in winter or if he is working hard, will promote early identification of potential trouble spots.

Areas that are most susceptible are the
- pasterns and heels; look for mud fever and cracked heels

Mud fever

- mane and tail for sweet itch and lice

Sweet itch

- girth and saddle area because of chafing tack

- back and sides in horses living out, rain scald

Rain scald

Even before bald areas appear the skin may be more sensitive to the finger-tip touch, and the hair starting to thin, and early recognition and treatment will prevent the condition becoming even worse.

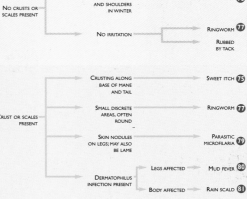

NO CRUSTS OR SCALES PRESENT	RUBBING MANE AND TAIL IN SUMMER	EARLY SWEET ITCH **75**
	RUBBING NECK AND SHOULDERS IN WINTER	LICE **76**
	NO IRRITATION	RINGWORM **77**
		RUBBED BY TACK
CRUST OR SCALES PRESENT	CRUSTING ALONG BASE OF MANE AND TAIL	SWEET ITCH **75**
	SMALL DISCRETE AREAS, OFTEN ROUND	RINGWORM **77**
	SKIN NODULES ON LEGS; MAY ALSO BE LAME	PARASITIC MICROFILARIA **79**
DERMATOPHILUS INFECTION PRESENT	LEGS AFFECTED	MUD FEVER **80**
	BODY AFFECTED	RAIN SCALD **81**

15

Lice do not live long off the horse. During the summer they are least active, and the symptoms tend to disappear; they are most active during cold weather in horses with a thick coat. Spread from horse to horse usually requires direct contact.

Lice breed in the long winter coat and feed on skin debris and body fluids. The itching they cause will make the horse or pony rub the most affected areas, usually the neck and shoulders, also the tail. The resulting bald or matted areas are seen in the mid to late winter

How is it treated?

Anti-parasitic dusting powders and **shampoos** are available, but they need weekly or monthly application because they rarely remove 100 per cent of the lice. Ivermectin wormers kill lice during the first twenty-four hours after their use. Clipping the coat removes the shelter used by the lice.

tive to the saliva irritation makes and tail. The hair es **serum** (see midges are active, d winter:

ing and may be a the horse. Besides uring those times daylight). In severe ecting the stable. etely remove the se they may trig- ch it will continue year.

mptoms are basi- lf. Patches of hair d shoulder areas

Ringworm **77**

Ringworm is a non-itching fungal skin disease. Because the **fungi** (usually members of the Trichophyton or Microsporum families) affect the skin and the base of the hairs, hairs break off at skin level, leaving bald areas. Typically these areas appear circular in shape, but ringworm does not always have such a convenient form. There may be small irregular areas anywhere on the body, or just occasional hairs might be affected.

Ringworm can survive for months or years in the environment because it forms spores that are resistant to extremes of temperature. Thus a horse may be infected for weeks or months before any symptoms appear. In fact horses will eventually cure themselves by developing an immunity to the fungus, and it is this fact that has led to the popularity of a number of folk remedies for the disease, which appear to work because some time after their use th These remedies include the applicatio noxious substances.

What is it?

The antibiotic griseofulvin given orally it has side effects. Anti-fungal wash hygiene must be employed for groomi stables and so on, to prevent the fungi

ENDOSCOPY

The flexible endoscope inserted through a nostril and down the respiratory system produces a video image on the screen

THIS TECHNIQUE usually involves using a bundle of flexible glass fibres to look inside the body. Originally it was the respiratory system that was investigated in this way, enabling the vet to examine all the way from the nostrils down to the entrance to the lungs. Endoscopes are also used to investigate the digestive system, passing down the oesophagus into the stomach. An arthroscope is a specialist kind of endoscope that is used for looking inside joints.

The endoscope consists of a powerful light source that is transmitted down one set of the fibres. The illuminated object is then viewed through a lens via another set of fibres. The outer flexible endoscopic tube also incorporates hollow channels that can be used to carry water or to remove fluids, and to enable tiny instruments to be inserted into the area that is being investigated. In the case of arthroscopy in particular there is a wide range of miniature power tools that can be manipulated in this way.

Video endoscopes or arthroscopes show the image on a screen, enlarged many times, rather than the vet having to hold the instrument up to their eye.

RADIOGRAPHY

Damage to a shoulder could be muscle-related, but radiography is able to detect whether or not it is something more serious, such as a bone fracture

RADIOGRAPHY was the first technique that let us look inside the body without surgery. It works by means of a beam of x-rays from the machine passes through the target and hits an x-ray plate. The film inside then has to be developed in a dark room, although in many cases the actual developing process is carried out automatically. The x-ray image is black, white and all the shades of grey. It records density rather than structure, so bone can be seen in great detail but muscles only show as an amorphous grey. Nevertheless a skilled radiographer can obtain a considerable amount of information about structures other than bone. Cartilage does not show on x-ray at all, however, which means that many arthritic changes do not show, either.

The horse's leg up to the knee and hock can be radiographed very well with mobile machines, but the rest of the body may need more powerful, fixed machines – and even then, the thickest part of the body, such as the spine, can be difficult to radiograph perfectly.

As when we take an ordinary photograph, the exposure used makes a big difference to the quality of the final x-ray. Vets can vary the kilovoltage that is used to generate the x-rays, affecting their penetration, and also the milliamperage, affecting the contrast of the image. There are now also digital x-ray machines that can alter the image electronically, at will.

Radiography can provide invaluable information about dental problems

146

147

FLOW CHARTS:
Interpreting Symptoms

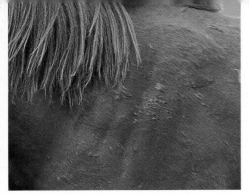
Dull coat, typical of a horse in poor condition

What makes you think your horse needs a blood test?

- He looks dull in his coat
- is off his food
- is lacking enthusiasm/sparkle in his work

What will a blood test tell me?

Blood consists of red and white cells and plasma. A red cell count (also PCV and haemoglobin) can show anaemia; a white cell count can indicate infection or disease in tissues (liver, heart, muscles, bone). Plasma is used to measure enzyme levels *eg* to detect muscle damage, and hormone levels *eg* in pregnancy and fertility tests. Blood can also be examined for unnatural substances, such as dope.

RED BLOOD CELLS
(p.177)

BLOOD SAMPLE
(p.150)

WHITE BLOOD CELLS
(p.177)

Taking a blood sample

Blood is collected by your vet from the jugular vein; it is important that the horse has not been exercised recently , and it should not be in an excited state, because this can distort the blood picture; for the same reason the horse should not be sedated.

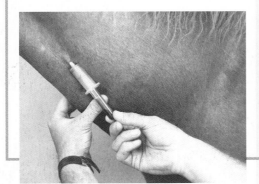

RAISED PCV →
→ DEHYDRATION (p.157)
→ EXCITEMENT /STRESS

NORMAL PCV → INCREASED MEAN CORPUSCULAR VOLUME → PREVIOUS ANAEMIA (p.164)

LOW PCV → LOW CELL NUMBERS

NEUTROPHILIA < NUMBERS (p.184)
→ LYMPHOCYTOSIS: INCREASED NUMBERS OF LYMPHOCYTES
→ EXCITEMENT
→ VIRAL INFECTION
→ MONOCYTOSIS → CHRONIC DISEASE
→ EOSINOPHILIA
→ ALLERGIC RESPONSE (p.137)
→ PARASITES 53

NEUTROPAENIA > NUMBERS
→ LYMPHOPAENIA
→ STRESS
→ STEROIDS (p.139)
→ LYMPHOSARCOMA 8
→ VIRAL INFECTION
→ EOSINOPAENIA → ACUTE INFECTION

11

Treating skin wounds

- Minor cuts/abrasions can be hosed with clean, cold water to reduce any swelling. Otherwise clean dirt out with cotton wool, clean water and a dilute antiseptic.
- Clip and remove any hairs around the wound. If you can't get it completely clean, cover it with a sterile dressing.
- Any pressure pad should not be applied for too long – certainly not more than an hour. Any bandage can cause problems by interfering with the blood flow, which can cause sloughing.
- If a wound is infected the surrounding area will be swollen, unusually warm, and painful to the touch. Make sure the horse's tetanus cover is up to date.
- Always allow as much air as possible to get to a wound: air is critical to healing, and if it is occluded, even through the use of antiseptic creams, anaerobic organisms proliferate. Therefore remove dressings at least every day, and if there is no infection, try to get them off altogether after three to four days.
- Proud flesh (granulation tissue) can be removed surgically or chemically with copper sulphate.
- Reduce the concentrate feed because the horse will not be in full work.
- Exercise judiciously: if possible walk in hand even the day after injury, to make the repair strong and able to withstand movement.

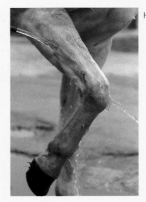

Hosing a wound to remove dirt and reduce swelling

NOT BLEEDING

BLEEDING

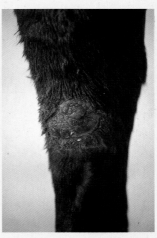

Proud flesh

→ INFECTED ⌐ LARGE OLD → SEEK VETERINARY
             WOUND   ATTENTION

          └ SMALL OLD → CLEAN DAILY.
             WOUND   (p.175)
                        APPLY ANTISEPTIC/
                        ANTIBIOTIC
                        (p.136, 141)

→ NOT INFECTED ⌐ FRESH WOUND → CLEAN DAILY
                  LESS THAN   (p.175)
                  2CM (1IN) LONG APPLY ANTISEPTIC/
                                  ANTIBIOTIC
                                  (p.136, 141)

               └ FRESH WOUND → SEEK VETERINARY
                  MORE THAN   ATTENTION
                  2CM (1IN) LONG

→ WOUND   → APPLY A
   SMALLER THAN   PRESSURE PAD
   2CM (1IN) LONG   (p.154)
                    CALL A VET IF
                    BLEEDING
                    CONTINUES

→ WOUND   → APPLY A   → SEEK VETERINARY
   LARGER THAN   PRESSURE PAD   ATTENTION
   2CM (1IN) LONG   IF POSSIBLE
                    (p.154)

Identifying bald areas

Regular inspection of the horse's skin, particularly in winter or if he is working hard, will promote early identification of potential trouble spots.

Areas that are most susceptible are the

- pasterns and heels; look for mud fever and cracked heels

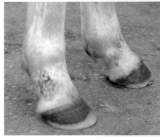

Mud fever

- mane and tail for sweet itch and lice

- girth and saddle area because of chafing tack

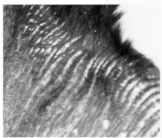

Sweet itch

- back and sides in horses living out, rain scald

Even before bald areas appear the skin may be more sensitive to the finger-tip touch, and the hair starting to thin, and early recognition and treatment will prevent the condition becoming even worse.

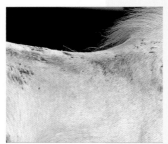

Rain scald

Ringworm

RUBBING MANE AND TAIL IN SUMMER → EARLY SWEET ITCH **75**

RUBBING NECK AND SHOULDERS IN WINTER → LICE **76**

NO IRRITATION → RINGWORM **77**

RUBBED BY TACK

CRUSTING ALONG BASE OF MANE AND TAIL → SWEET ITCH **75**

SMALL DISCRETE AREAS, OFTEN ROUND → RINGWORM **77**

SKIN NODULES ON LEGS; MAY ALSO BE LAME → PARASITIC MICROFILARIA **79**

DERMATOPHILUS INFECTION PRESENT → LEGS AFFECTED → MUD FEVER **80**

BODY AFFECTED → RAIN SCALD **81**

When to worry about swelling:

- Swelling caused by a snake bite may be toxic, so call a vet
- Swelling on an eyelid might lead to infection and lead to problems involving the eye itself, so check it daily
- Swelling on the head might indicate tooth problems (see p.64-6 and p.145), sinus disease (see p.89) or bone injuries: seek professional help
- Any swelling that departs significantly from the horse's normal shape
- Swelling associated with lameness
- Swelling of the lower limb may indicate a problem further up the leg that is interfering with the circulation; or infection (pus) in the foot

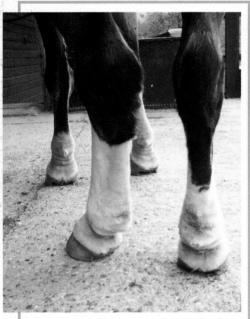

Swollen leg due to infection associated with mud fever. White, non-pigmented areas are especially susceptible

SOFT
REMAINS PITTED AFTER PRESSURE FROM A FINGER

CONTAINS FLUID

WARM, PAINFUL

FIRM
NON-PAINFUL

CONTAINS SPECIFIC AREAS

HARD
CONTAINS SPECIFIC AREAS

OEDEMA ⟶ INSECT BITE **14**

⟶ DAMAGE TO BLOOD VESSEL

WARM, PAINFUL ⟶ CONTAINS PUS (p.136) ⟶ ABSCESS **15**

COOL, NON-PAINFUL ⟶ CONTAINS BLOOD ⟶ HAEMATOMA **16**

⟶ SLOW-GROWING ⟶ CYST (p.186)

LOCALISED INFECTION ⟶ CELLULITIS (p.186)

POSSIBLE TUMOUR (p.140) ⟶ SARCOID **18**

⟶ MELANOMA **19**

ASSOCIATED WITH PREVIOUS WOUND ⟶ SCAR TISSUE (p.186)

⟶ GRANULATION TISSUE (p.12)

HERNIA (p.165)

⟶ BONY EXOSTOSIS, *eg* SPLINT **17**

Identifying the cause:

■ If there is a dental problem, the horse will 'quid' – allow half-masticated food to drop from his mouth; he is probably uncomfortable with his bit, too.

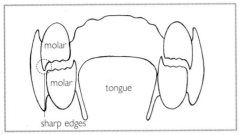

Wear on the molars can lead to sharp edges appearing

Otherwise he may look well with a shiny coat, bright eye.

■ He might not like the food – generally concentrates – so leave out the different components of the horse's feed (nuts/oats/ barley/sugar beet) until you establish what it is he doesn't like. Many horses don't like/won't eat supplements/ powders in feed. Some horses eat better in the afternoon: they won't eat breakfast – so feed later, eg after exercise at, say, 11am/midday; then at 5/6pm; and at 10/11pm at night.

■ Off colour: dull in coat and eye; will look 'droopy'; anxious, biting/looking at sides if colic, also getting up and down; maybe hot/sweaty. Azoturia: stiff over loins; won't move.

NORMAL IN OTHER RESPECTS

OFF COLOUR

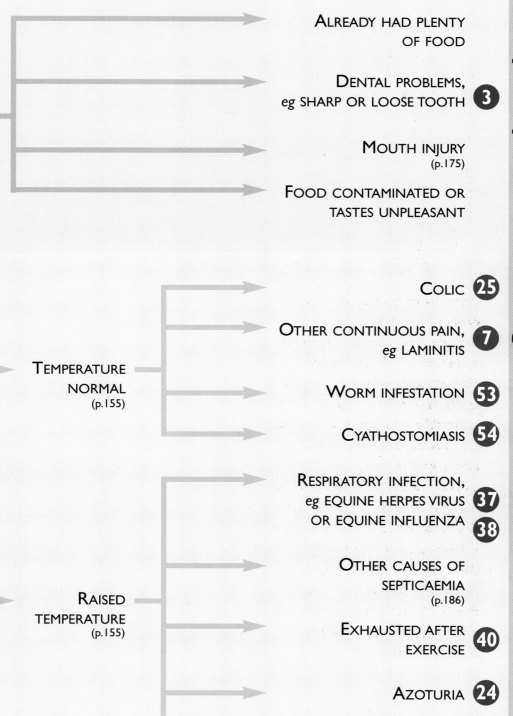

ALREADY HAD PLENTY OF FOOD

DENTAL PROBLEMS, *eg* SHARP OR LOOSE TOOTH **3**

MOUTH INJURY (p.175)

FOOD CONTAMINATED OR TASTES UNPLEASANT

COLIC **25**

OTHER CONTINUOUS PAIN, *eg* LAMINITIS **7**

WORM INFESTATION **53**

CYATHOSTOMIASIS **54**

TEMPERATURE NORMAL (p.155)

RESPIRATORY INFECTION, *eg* EQUINE HERPES VIRUS **37** OR EQUINE INFLUENZA **38**

OTHER CAUSES OF SEPTICAEMIA (p.186)

EXHAUSTED AFTER EXERCISE **40**

AZOTURIA **24**

RAISED TEMPERATURE (p.155)

MILD COLIC **25**

19

How might I avoid colic?

Colic is digestive upset, so avoid situations that might cause it. This might occur:

- When a horse's diet changes suddenly: eg when he is brought back into training and stabled after a long spell at grass: make any changes in diet gradual – feed hay for the first two or three days, introduce hard feed in small amounts (1–2lb), increase gradually; keep turning out daily but for less time each day over a period of, say, 2–3 weeks.
- If he bolts his food: add chaff to his feed to slow down his speed of eating, or feed coarse mix.
- If he is fed too much at any one time: feed according to workload and bodyweight – take advice, weigh the feed: if too much, divide the amount into five or six feeds to be given over any 24 hours.
- If he is stabled for very long periods: give feed at regular intervals throughout the 24 hours; never leave him without fibre for longer than an hour.
- If he is given poor quality forage, because indigestible roughage leads to gas production: make sure hay, haylage are of good quality, and as we have seen, also in constant supply.
- If he feels stressed: eg when travelling: make frequent breaks in a (long) journey; if he is left on his own: find him a companion; if he is hot/stressed after a workout: cool him down/unwind him gradually.
- If he is not wormed properly.

Violent rolling can be an indication of colic

TEMPERATURE NORMAL
(p.155)

TEMPERATURE RAISED
(p.155)

A companion can help a horse overcome stress

MEMBRANES AROUND
EYES NORMAL → MILD IMPACTION **25**

MEMBRANES AROUND
EYES JAUNDICED
(p.180) → IMPACTION OF SMALL
INTESTINE **25**

MAY BE ASSOCIATED WITH
GRASS SICKNESS **26**

PAIN INTERMITTENT → MILD SPASMODIC COLIC **25**

GASTRIC TYMPANY **25**

MEMBRANES AROUND
EYES BLUISH IN COLOUR → GASTRIC IMPACTION **25**

TYMPANITIC COLIC **25**

NOT ROLLING MUCH, BUT
LOUD BOWEL SOUNDS → SPASMODIC COLIC **25**

INTERMITTENT PAIN
BECOMES CONTINUOUS → TYMPANITIC COLIC **25**

VERY ACUTE PAIN → DISPLACEMENT OF PART OF
INTESTINES, SO-CALLED
'TWISTED GUT' **25**

Check the quality of the forage you are giving to your horse

Management practices as a cause of diarrhoea:

- Avoid sudden and extreme changes in diet; this could be from a very poor to a very rich pasture, eg when bringing a mare home from stud, where the land is often grazed bare; or a sudden reduction in fibre (forage), which will cause the associated organisms to disappear from the gut, so that food eaten subsequently won't be digested.
- Never feed contaminated silage.
- Never feed excessive protein (as a supplement).
- Have a proper worming regime that involves treating all the yard at the same time.
- See page 157.

HORSE STILL APPEARS WELL

HORSE RAPIDLY BECOMES ILL

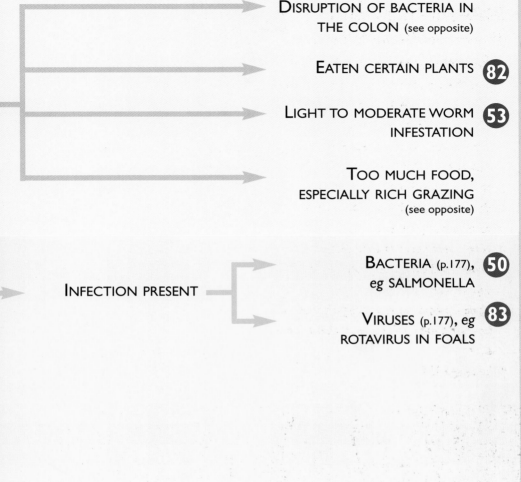

DISRUPTION OF BACTERIA IN
THE COLON (see opposite)

EATEN CERTAIN PLANTS **82**

LIGHT TO MODERATE WORM **53**
INFESTATION

TOO MUCH FOOD,
ESPECIALLY RICH GRAZING
(see opposite)

INFECTION PRESENT

BACTERIA (p.177), **50**
eg SALMONELLA

VIRUSES (p.177), eg **83**
ROTAVIRUS IN FOALS

ENDOTOXIC SHOCK **51**
(COLITIS X)

NO INFECTION PRESENT   SEVERE WORM INFESTATION **53**

eg CYATHOSTOMIASIS **54**

Signs of lameness

■ Horse stands awkwardly, may rest a front leg, or consistently rests the same back leg.

■ Obvious lameness will be seen when the horse moves, even at walk.

■ Trotting the horse in hand is the clearest way to reveal less obvious lameness. This should be done on a safe, flat surface with a separate observer on hand.

Best conditions for checking lameness

■ The surface should be level; not stony or muddy/slippery.

■ Trot the horse up on a loose rein.

Identifying the lame leg

When a lame horse is trotted he will nod when his sound foreleg hits the ground because it is taking more weight.

When trotted away from the observer the lame horse's hips will dip noticeably lower on the side of the sound hind leg as it hits the ground.

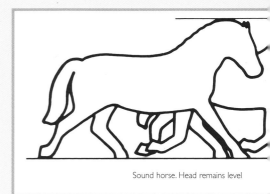

Sound horse. Head remains level

HEAD NODDING, TAIL STEADY WHEN TROTTED IN STRAIGHT LINE

TAIL SINKING, HEAD STEADY WHEN TROTTED IN STRAIGHT LINE

Lame horse. Head sinks to the ground as good leg hits the ground.

HEAD NODS WHEN LEFT FORELEG HITS THE GROUND ⟹ LAME RIGHT FORE

HEAD NODS WHEN RIGHT FORELEG HITS THE GROUND ⟹ LAME LEFT FORE

HINDQUARTERS SINK WHEN LEFT HIND LEG HITS THE GROUND ⟹ LAME RIGHT HIND

HINDQUARTERS SINK WHEN RIGHT HIND LEG HITS THE GROUND ⟹ LAME LEFT HIND

Locating lameness

- Examine the lame limb for swelling, heat, pain or muscle wasting, starting at the foot, where the majority of lameness is sited, and working upwards.
- With slight lameness the horse won't necessarily nod, but typically you will see an altered flight pattern. Thus in shoulder lameness the limb will rotate outwards or inwards, and the stride, from the side view, will track short. In upper hind limb lameness the horse will show a marked physical effort in lifting the leg; look for swellings or wasting at pelvic level.
- Some forms of lameness are more obvious going up or down an incline.
- Check that the horse isn't striking into himself – brushing, speedy cutting, forging – this can make him very lame, particularly behind, and the resultant bruising can make him susceptible for a long time. Get your farrier to check the foot balance (p.161); wear brushing boots. Get his back checked.

PAIN ON HOOF PRESSURE

Hoof tester

NO PAIN ON HOOF PRESSURE

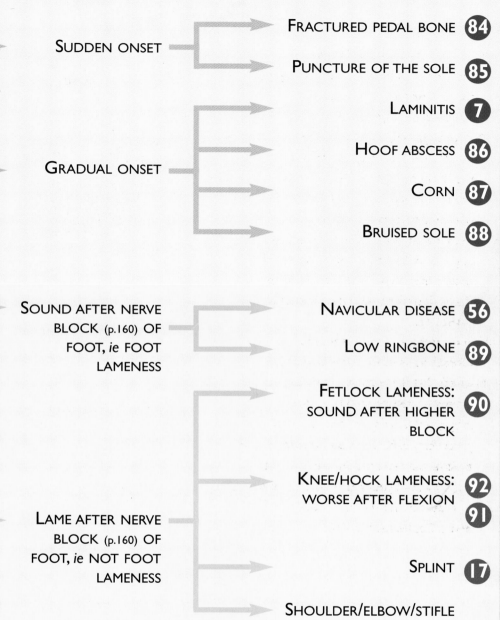

SUDDEN ONSET ——— FRACTURED PEDAL BONE **84**

PUNCTURE OF THE SOLE **85**

LAMINITIS **7**

GRADUAL ONSET ——— HOOF ABSCESS **86**

CORN **87**

BRUISED SOLE **88**

SOUND AFTER NERVE BLOCK (p.160) OF FOOT, *ie* FOOT LAMENESS ——— NAVICULAR DISEASE **56**

LOW RINGBONE **89**

FETLOCK LAMENESS: SOUND AFTER HIGHER BLOCK **90**

KNEE/HOCK LAMENESS: WORSE AFTER FLEXION **92** **91**

LAME AFTER NERVE BLOCK (p.160) OF FOOT, *ie* NOT FOOT LAMENESS ——— SPLINT **17**

SHOULDER/ELBOW/STIFLE LAMENESS (p.26): ONLY IF ALL OTHERS EXHAUSTED

Why is my horse lame?

Tendon injuries

Tendon injuries will show pain on finger pressure. Passive filling in a lower limb could be caused by a graze or wound further up the leg; it can also result from digestive problems, or lymphangitis.

Filling of a lower part of the leg such as this may be a sign of a wound further up the limb

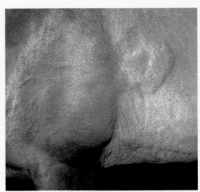

SWELLING PITS WITH PRESSURE (OEDEMA)

Pus in the foot

Pus in the foot (p.136) will often cause the leg to fill, and when this happens it often looks as though the tendon itself is injured; finger pressure on the tendon and a hoof tester on the foot will indicate the true site of pain. If infection is present the swelling will continue increasing in severity.

SWELLING DOES NOT PIT WITH PRESSURE

MAINLY
CANNON AREA

MAINLY BACK
OF LEG → TENDON OR **60**
LIGAMENT SPRAIN

MAINLY ON SIDE
OF LEG → SPLINT BONE **17**
FRACTURE
(POSSIBLY
INFECTED)

ASSOCIATED WITH
KNEE OR BACK
PROBLEM → RESULT OF
DISRUPTION OF
CIRCULATION
(p.143)

WHOLE LEG
AFFECTED → LYMPHANGITIS **62**

LIVER DISEASE **55**

SYSTEMIC PROBLEM
WITH OTHER PART
OF BODY AFFECTED → PURPURA **63**
HAEMORRHAGIA

ABNORMAL
PROTEIN
METABOLISM

LOCALISED
INFECTION → PUS IN THE FOOT **85**

PUNCTURE
WOUND (p.171)

INFECTED BONE **17**
FRACTURE

Maintaining strong, healthy horn

Good feeding is critical in maintaining strong, healthy horn; and routine care and sensible management will help prevent deterioration in hoof quality. Thus horses left standing outside in wet, muddy conditions will often suffer a general softening of the horn; and conversely, horses left out on hard, dry ground with no shoes on will usually come in with cracked, split hooves.

Sandcrack

Unshod hoof showing natural wear

OVERGROWN HOOVES
BREAK AWAY

DAMP CONDITIONS MAY
SOFTEN HORN → THRUSH **20**

POOR QUALITY FARRIERY
(p.161), ESPECIALLY THE
ATTACHMENT OF SHOES

BIOTIN DEFICIENCY **21**

D.L. METHIONINE
DEFICIENCY **21**

EXCESSIVE CLEANING OR
RASPING OF HOOF WALL,
REMOVING PROTECTIVE
BARRIER

OVER-USE OF WATERPROOF
SEALANTS ON HOOF

LACK OF PROTECTION FROM
DRYING IN HOT WEATHER

Horse not standing

A horse that is unable to stand for any length of time is in serious trouble, as its large body mass and the structure of its digestive system will rapidly cause its whole body system to fail.

Slings may be used as artificial support.

Cast horse

If it is cast on its back against a wall/bank it will need to be rolled back over, by grasping hold of/roping the lateral fore- and hindlegs that are underneath/against the wall. A horse that has gone down and won't – as opposed to can't – get up (been winded/cast/bogged/caught up) will often be encouraged to get to its feet if it is rolled onto its other side in this way.

UNWILLING TO STAND

UNABLE TO STAND

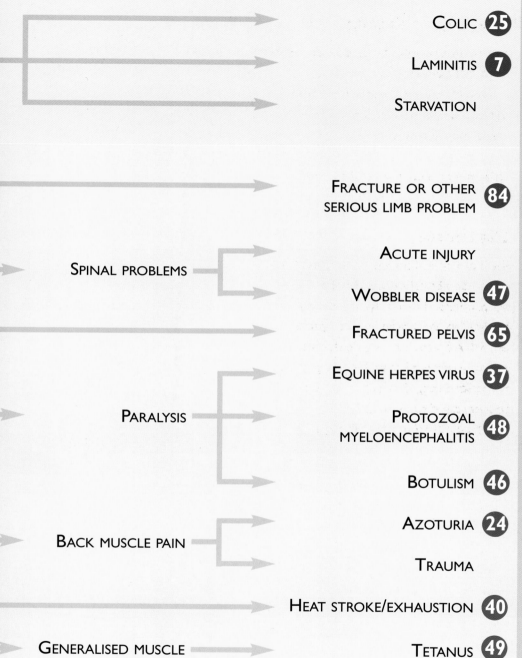

COLIC **25**

LAMINITIS **7**

STARVATION

FRACTURE OR OTHER SERIOUS LIMB PROBLEM **84**

SPINAL PROBLEMS

ACUTE INJURY

WOBBLER DISEASE **47**

FRACTURED PELVIS **65**

EQUINE HERPES VIRUS **37**

PARALYSIS

PROTOZOAL MYELOENCEPHALITIS **48**

BOTULISM **46**

AZOTURIA **24**

BACK MUSCLE PAIN

TRAUMA

HEAT STROKE/EXHAUSTION **40**

GENERALISED MUSCLE SPASM

TETANUS **49**

Laminitis

- This is a very painful condition that can involve all four feet of the horse. It is associated with inflammation (and possible death) of the sensitive fold of tissue that join the horse of the hoof to the pedal bone.

- Laminitis can occur due to a number of causes, but is commonly associated with eating lush green grass or other herbage. A horse or pony restricted to an area of very short grass can still get laminitis. The grass might still be growing very rapidly and be very sweet and lush, and the horse might be eating it as fast as it grows, in the process getting large quantities of grass.

- Horses with laminitis need to stand still or lie down in order to reduce the leverage forces on their feet during movement, causing separation of the hoof from the bone. Stable rest, preferably on a sand bed, is essential. This goes against the centuries old tradition of forcing horses with laminitis to walk around, but it does have solid science behind it.

ENDOTOXINS FROM GUT
(p.139)

PAIN

ROTATION OR SINKING OF
THE PEDAL BONE

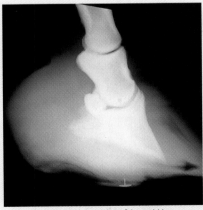

An x-ray showing rotation of the pedal bone away from the hoof wall

TOXINS FROM INFECTION
(p.157)

RELEASE OF
VASO-CONSTRICTORS
WHICH REDUCE BLOOD
FLOW TO THE FOOT

BLOOD SHUNTS AROUND
THE CORONET AND BACK
UP THE LEG

ANOXIA OR LACK
OF OXYGEN
(p.183)

SUSCEPTIBILITY TO FURTHER
EPISODES

DEGENERATION
OF THE LAMINAE

MAY HEAL SLOWLY, BUT
TAKES SEVERAL MONTHS

RECOVERY

7

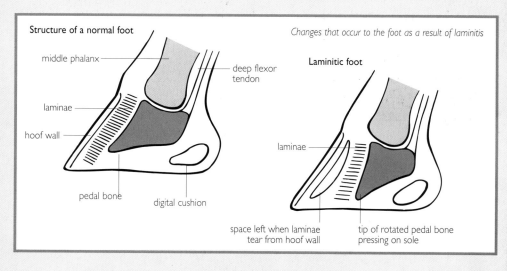

Structure of a normal foot

Changes that occur to the foot as a result of laminitis

middle phalanx

deep flexor
tendon

Laminitic foot

laminae

hoof wall

laminae

pedal bone

digital cushion

space left when laminae
tear from hoof wall

tip of rotated pedal bone
pressing on sole

Checking for Back Pain

When a horse's performance deteriorates, one of the first things to check is his back. Signs of spinal pain might be:

- stiffness and restricted movement
- tender when touched over specific area – could be neck, back, loins or quarters
- muscular spasm; dips the back when mounted ('cold back')
- steps short on affected side; will find stepping backwards difficult
- has problems when turning short, finding foot placement difficult, prefers to change directly from the walk to canter and vice versa without trotting
- Remember that not all poor performance is the result of back pain.

Checking for back pain

Watch the horse's action closely, and run a daily check by gently feeling along the spine for pain that results from light fingertip pressure; sudden changes in reaction may be significant. Check the horse's ability and willingness to move its neck through a range of movements – such as touching its shoulder with its muzzle. Note any change in movement when riding – particularly loss of elasticity, looseness. The back and pelvic muscles should be symmetrical.

PRIMARY BACK PROBLEM

HORSE IS LAME BUT HAS SECONDARY BACK PAIN

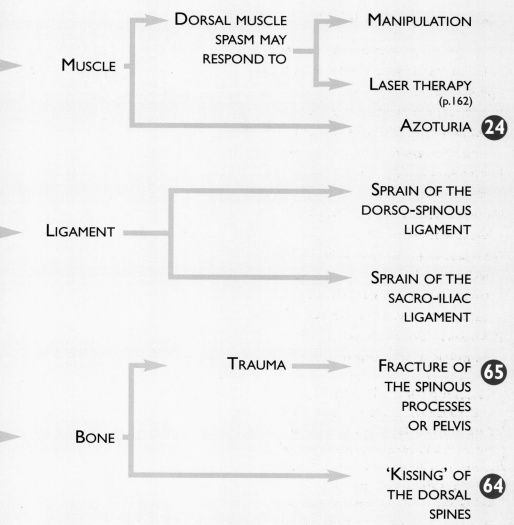

MUSCLE

DORSAL MUSCLE
SPASM MAY
RESPOND TO

MANIPULATION

LASER THERAPY
(p.162)

AZOTURIA **24**

LIGAMENT

SPRAIN OF THE
DORSO-SPINOUS
LIGAMENT

SPRAIN OF THE
SACRO-ILIAC
LIGAMENT

BONE

TRAUMA

FRACTURE OF **65**
THE SPINOUS
PROCESSES
OR PELVIS

'KISSING' OF **64**
THE DORSAL
SPINES

PAIN WILL
RECUR UNTIL
PRIMARY
LAMENESS IS
ELIMINATED

Staggering horse

In maintaining a horse's good health and working ability, prevention is always better than cure.

■ A rider/driver should recognise signs of extreme tiredness in his horse, and not drive it to the point of exhaustion.

■ Poisonous plants (especially ragwort) should be pulled up from all pastureland and destroyed before horses are turned out/grass is cut for hay.

■ Good stable management can help reduce the chances of azoturia: thus cut down concentrate feed before any rest period; and cool a horse down properly if he is hot after a workout, walking or trotting slowly.

METABOLIC PROBLEMS

Ragwort

NERVOUS SYSTEM PROBLEMS
(p.179)

Be very careful when feeding bagged haylage/horsehage: if the wrapping is damaged and there are signs of mould/a bad smell/it feels wet and slimy/it is heating up – don't feed it!

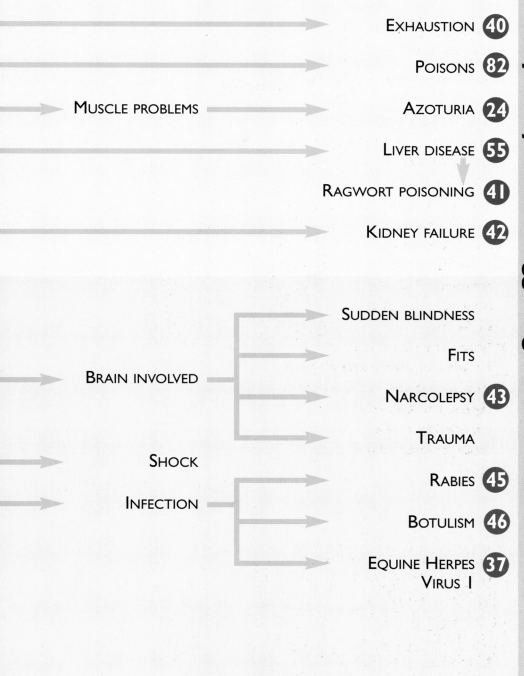

EXHAUSTION 40

POISONS 82

MUSCLE PROBLEMS · AZOTURIA 24

LIVER DISEASE 55

RAGWORT POISONING 41

KIDNEY FAILURE 42

BRAIN INVOLVED

SUDDEN BLINDNESS

FITS

NARCOLEPSY 43

TRAUMA

SHOCK

INFECTION

RABIES 45

BOTULISM 46

EQUINE HERPES 37
VIRUS I

SPINAL PROBLEMS · WOBBLER SYNDROME 47

Causes of azoturia

(also known as 'tying up', see p.79):

- Can be caused by particular types of feed or ways of feeding. A day off work or with reduced exercise is a common trigger factor.
- Can be caused by insufficient warm-up before fast exercise: at least 20 mins of brisk trotting; and if he is not cooled down properly afterwards: 10–20 mins of active walk. Give electrolytes to help reduce blood acidity, a causative factor in azoturia.

What to do if he ties up:

- Cover with a rug and keep warm.
- If he can walk and you're not too far from home/a stable, walk him there and call the vet.
- If he is in acute pain, do not walk him, but rug him, call a vet, and arrange to box him home, if he can be loaded/is fit enough to travel.
- If he can't move, keep him warm, call a vet, and you will have to wait until he is fit enough to move.
- Once home, cut back on concentrates straightaway; give a small mash and meadow hay.
- If possible, walk him out next day for a bite of grass; long-term stabling/box rest will be necessary.
- His return to work will be based on how he copes, and why he tied up.
- Critically assess his diet: as work is resumed, feed simple concentrates in carefully monitored quantities, and meadow hay.
- Strapping will help disperse muscle lesions; also physiotherapy.

CARBOHYDRATE METABOLISM
(p.186)

ELECTROLYTE METABOLISM
(p.143)

HORMONE METABOLISM
(p.183)

EXERCISE CONSTANT → **OVERALL EXCESS CARBOHYDRATE**

→ **VARYING FEED LEVELS**

VARYING LEVELS EXERCISE → **CONSTANT FEED**

→ **VARYING FEED LEVELS**

SODIUM → **INADEQUATE INTAKE**

→ **RAISED REQUIREMENT**

CALCIUM → **INADEQUATE INTAKE**

→ **RAISED REQUIREMENT**

MAGNESIUM → **INADEQUATE INTAKE**

→ **RAISED REQUIREMENT**

THYROID DYSFUNCTION

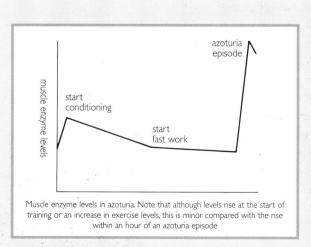

Muscle enzyme levels in azoturia. Note that although levels rise at the start of training or an increase in exercise levels, this is minor compared with the rise within an hour of an azoturia episode

Improving the environment

Good stable management can reduce the symptoms of many respiratory problems, so that it may be possible to ride the horse usefully again:

- There must be adequate air in the stable, without draughts.
- The atmosphere must be dust free: remove cobwebs, dust, any hay and/or straw residue.
- Use dust-free bedding – maybe paper on rubber matting.
- Feed good quality, clean haylage rather than hay.
- If really badly affected the horse could live out, with a New Zealand rug and access to a shelter.
- In extreme cases the vet may provide drugs to relieve the symptoms and make riding possible.

AT REST

Stable hygiene is a factor in controlling many health problems, respiratory conditions among them

Shavings are a more dust-free alternative to standard straw

ONLY DURING/AFTER EXERCISE (p.185)

COPD **28**

HEART FAILURE **29**

PNEUMONIA **30**

AIRWAY INADEQUATE
FOR LOW DEMANDS
FOR AIR

ACUTE ALLERGIC
REACTION **31**

TUMOUR (p.168) OF
RESPIRATORY SYSTEM

LARYNGEAL PARALYSIS **10**

LESS SEVERE FORMS OF ALL
THE ABOVE

PAIN FROM
NON-RESPIRATORY SOURCES

AIRWAY ADEQUATE FOR
LOW DEMANDS FOR
AIR, BUT NOT FOR
INCREASED DEMAND

NASAL POLYP BLOCKING
AIRWAY **32**

SOFT PALATE PROBLEMS **13**

PULMONARY
HAEMORRHAGE **33**

TRACHEAL COLLAPSE/
BLOCKAGE **34**

Assessing respiratory noise

In assessing whether the respiratory noise will
compromise the horse's performance, it is useful to
know his normal breathing rate: at rest this is about
10–12 breaths per minute; at the gallop this can be as
high as 150 per minute (see also p.178). Even a 5 or 10
per cent reduction in air intake during peak exercise will
be seriously inhibiting, and might even lead to internal
bleeding. It is therefore essential to identify why the
horse is making a noise and to assess how inhibiting an
influence it is.

(see also p.178)

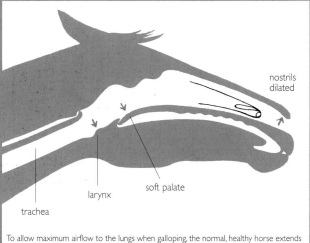

nostrils
dilated

soft palate

larynx

trachea

To allow maximum airflow to the lungs when galloping, the normal, healthy horse extends
his head and dilates his nostrils. The soft palate, larynx and trachea are streamlined in
order not to interfere with the free passage of air.

INSPIRATION

EXPIRATION

MAY ALSO
COUGH WHEN
EATING →→→→→→→→→→→ EPIGLOTTIC
ENTRAPMENT **9**

ROARING
(p.185) →→→→→→→→→→→ LARYNGEAL
HEMIPLEGIA **10**

INVOLVES
NOSTRIL →→→ ┌→ COLLAPSE OF ALAR
FOLD OF NOSTRIL **12**
└→ ATHEROMA OF
FALSE NOSTRIL **11**

ABNORMAL ┌→ LOUD
GURGLING → DORSAL
DISPLACEMENT OF
SOFT PALATE **13**
└→ MAY ALSO
COUGH
WHEN EATING → EPIGLOTTIC
ENTRAPMENT **9**

NORMAL ┌→ HIGH
BLOWING → VIBRATION OF THE
FALSE NOSTRIL
└→ SNORTING → CLEARANCE OF
RESPIRATORY MUCUS

Assessing Inflamed Membranes

Nasal discharges may be accompanied by inflamed membranes of the eye and nose, the character of which will help in diagnosis. Thus besides the watery discharge of some viral conditions, the membranes show varying degrees of abnormal colouring.

Note that nasal membranes are normally richly coloured after exercise, so an assessment should not be made after work, but some hours later when the horse has cooled down and relaxed.

Thick nasal discharge

Clear, watery nasal discharge

ACUTE
(SHORT TERM)

CHRONIC
(LONG TERM)

CONTAINS BLOOD → PULMONARY HAEMORRHAGE **33**

→ ETHMOID HAEMATOMA **39**

CLEAR MUCUS → VIRAL INFECTION → EQUINE INFLUENZA **38**

→ EQUINE HERPES VIRUS **37**

THICK MUCUS → BACTERIAL INFECTION (MAYBE SECONDARY) → STRANGLES **36**

→ OTHER STREPTOCOCCI

→ INFECTION OF SINUSES **35**

→ GUTTURAL POUCH INFECTION **5**

→ COPD **28**

→ NASAL FOREIGN BODY (p.166)

Improving Management

Do not just rely on drugs to treat a cough: the answer lies rather in improving yard management, and making sure the horse has every chance of clearing any infection through his own natural resistance. His defensive mechanisms will not be able to do their job well in the face of a poor diet, worm infestation or lax hygiene. The following factors will lower resistance and leave the horse vulnerable to coughs, chills and infection:

■ Being kept stabled all the time, without regular exercise

■ Being kept in cold, draughty, damp conditions

■ Poor hygiene, causing a rank-smelling atmosphere

■ Improper or inadequate feeding

■ Worms and other parasites

■ Overwork

■ Failing to dry a horse properly after exercise

■ Long journeys, as they may cause exhaustion and dehydration

Thus tighten up your basic stable care, and he might not succomb to a cough

TEMPERATURE NORMAL
(p.155)

TEMPERATURE RAISED
(THIS MAY ONLY BE FOR
A SHORT TIME)
(p.155)

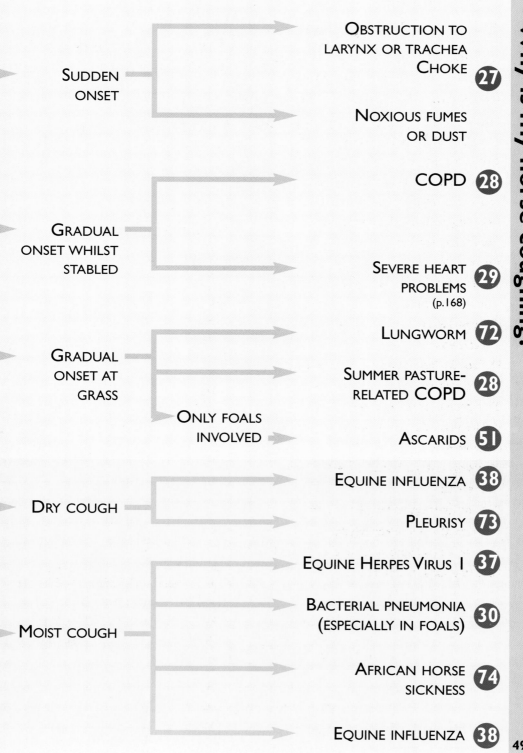

SUDDEN ONSET

OBSTRUCTION TO LARYNX OR TRACHEA CHOKE 27

NOXIOUS FUMES OR DUST

GRADUAL ONSET WHILST STABLED

COPD 28

SEVERE HEART PROBLEMS (p.168) 29

GRADUAL ONSET AT GRASS

LUNGWORM 72

SUMMER PASTURE-RELATED COPD 28

ONLY FOALS INVOLVED

ASCARIDS 51

DRY COUGH

EQUINE INFLUENZA 38

PLEURISY 73

MOIST COUGH

EQUINE HERPES VIRUS 1 37

BACTERIAL PNEUMONIA (ESPECIALLY IN FOALS) 30

AFRICAN HORSE SICKNESS 74

EQUINE INFLUENZA 38

Coping with head shaking

Idiopathic head shaking is a real problem in the ridden horse. It appears to be worse in warm humid conditions during summer, aggravated by the presence of flying summer mites.

A nose fringe or net is generally a calming influence, and the wearing of such fringes is currently permitted in most competitions.

A bridle that is fitted too tight will cause a horse to shake his head: if the bit is too high, or the browband/ headpiece/noseband (particularly a flash or a grakle) are too tight he will show obvious signs of discomfort.

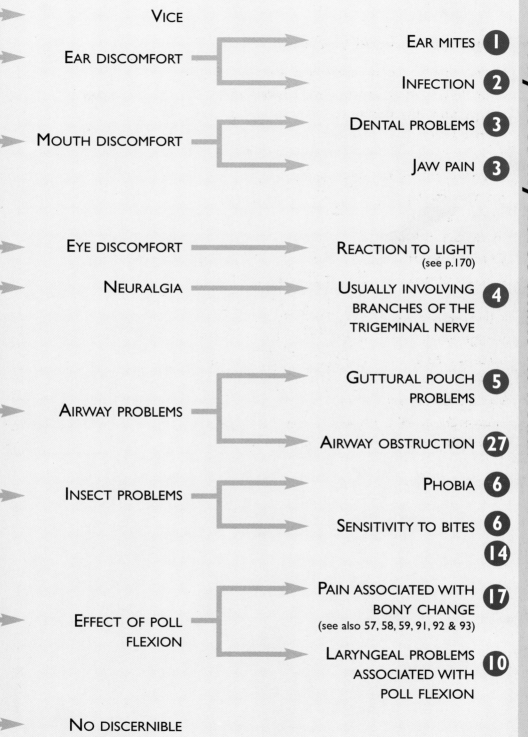

VICE

EAR DISCOMFORT — EAR MITES **1**
— INFECTION **2**

MOUTH DISCOMFORT — DENTAL PROBLEMS **3**
— JAW PAIN **3**

EYE DISCOMFORT — REACTION TO LIGHT
(see p.170)

NEURALGIA — USUALLY INVOLVING
BRANCHES OF THE
TRIGEMINAL NERVE **4**

AIRWAY PROBLEMS — GUTTURAL POUCH
PROBLEMS **5**
— AIRWAY OBSTRUCTION **27**

INSECT PROBLEMS — PHOBIA **6**
— SENSITIVITY TO BITES **6**
14

EFFECT OF POLL
FLEXION — PAIN ASSOCIATED WITH
BONY CHANGE **17**
(see also 57, 58, 59, 91, 92 & 93)
— LARYNGEAL PROBLEMS
ASSOCIATED WITH
POLL FLEXION **10**

NO DISCERNIBLE
CAUSE: IDIOPATHIC

Recognising signs of weight loss

It is important to recognise signs of weight change as early as possible: by the time a condition is well advanced, the weight could be dropping off the horse rapidly. Watch for:

- a reduction in girth measurement (use a proper weighband – ordinary string can stretch)
- the quarters and loins less rounded
- thinner over the ribs
- lighter in the neck
- possibly starey coat
- the skin may become dry and tight

(left) A lean but fit horse showing all the signs of good health, including a shining coat and alert eye

(below) Emaciaton is obvious in this case

A high standard of hygiene in the feed room is essential, and all the more so if the horse is not eating up and so losing condition:

feeding utensils should be scrupulously clean – buckets, scoops, mangers – and all feedstuffs of impeccable quality.

Good quality haylage/silage is an excellent body-builder; otherwise keep feedstuffs quite simple – straight grains, and/or one type of formulated cube or concentrate mix. Too much choice, and too much at one time, may in itself put a horse off its feed.

EATING

NOT EATING

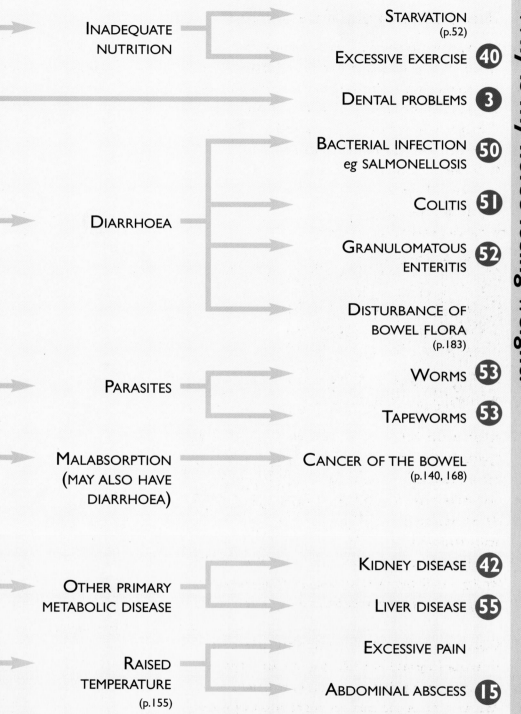

INADEQUATE NUTRITION

STARVATION (p.52)

EXCESSIVE EXERCISE **40**

DENTAL PROBLEMS **3**

DIARRHOEA

BACTERIAL INFECTION *eg* SALMONELLOSIS **50**

COLITIS **51**

GRANULOMATOUS ENTERITIS **52**

DISTURBANCE OF BOWEL FLORA (p.183)

PARASITES

WORMS **53**

TAPEWORMS **53**

MALABSORPTION (MAY ALSO HAVE DIARRHOEA)

CANCER OF THE BOWEL (p.140, 168)

OTHER PRIMARY METABOLIC DISEASE

KIDNEY DISEASE **42**

LIVER DISEASE **55**

RAISED TEMPERATURE (p.155)

EXCESSIVE PAIN

ABDOMINAL ABSCESS **15**

The effects of sweating

Sweating results in the loss of heat, fluid, salts and protein. The fluid, salts and protein will need to be replaced at a later time; this process can be helped by giving electrolytes. It is natural for a horse to sweat during and after exercise to disperse heat, but a fit horse produces less heat and so sweats less than an unfit horse. It is the evaporation of the sweat which cools the horse, not its production. When the horse's coat has been dried off it should be groomed to restore the fluffiness that provides insulation against cold. During strenuous exercise the horse produces a lot of heat – up to fifty times that produced at rest. In hot weather it may be necessary to cool him down with buckets of water and ice. Cold water should be applied liberally over the body, and his quarters especially: do this for 30 seconds, then walk him around for 30 seconds; this will increase the skin's blood flow, and its movement helps evaporation.

Sweating during and after exercise is quite normal, but profuse sweating at other times could be a sign of illness

ABSENT

INCREASED LOCALLY

INCREASED GENERALLY

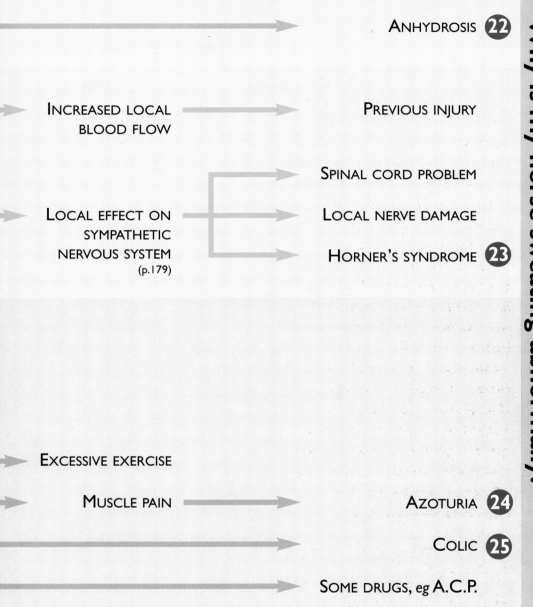

ANHYDROSIS 22

INCREASED LOCAL
BLOOD FLOW

PREVIOUS INJURY

SPINAL CORD PROBLEM

LOCAL EFFECT ON
SYMPATHETIC
NERVOUS SYSTEM
(p.179)

LOCAL NERVE DAMAGE

HORNER'S SYNDROME 23

EXCESSIVE EXERCISE

MUSCLE PAIN

AZOTURIA 24

COLIC 25

SOME DRUGS, eg A.C.P.

GRASS SICKNESS 26

Something hurts

The most usual reason that a horse's performance deteriorates is because something is hurting, and it is important that the individual rider knows how his horse moves naturally – when it is fit and sound – so as to recognise any change from normal. He can then investigate straightaway, adjusting exercise to help bring the damaged part back into good health as soon as possible.

The following non-specific problems can cause poor performance:

- Badly fitting tack – his saddle may have started to rub/pinch if he has changed shape in training.
- Not warming up properly before exercise, particularly when the weather is cold.
- Schooling a horse that is simply not fit enough, together with not understanding the need for muscles to recover from work.
- All-weather surfaces that are slippery, have insufficient grip.
- Working on inclines that are really too steep, and working too fast.
- Over-training – too much pace, or too many intervals, and not enough recovery time.
- Demanding too much from the horse – maybe too many competitions.
- A diet that has a deleterious effect on muscle metabolism and increases fibre fragility, perhaps because of mineral imbalances.

LAME
(p.26-7)

FAST RESPIRATORY RATE AFTER EXERCISE, UNUSUALLY FAST HEART/PULSE RATE (p.178)

Over-training and the constant demands of too many competitions can push a horse to breaking point

INADEQUATE OR INCORRECT TRAINING

OLDER HORSE
(6+ YEARS) → SPAVIN **91**

NAVICULAR DISEASE **56**

YOUNGER HORSE
(2–6 YEARS) → SORE SHINS **57**

OCD **58**

ALL AGES → SMALL CHIP FRACTURES
OF BONE **59**

SPLINT **17**

PRIMARY RESPIRATORY
PROBLEM → RESPIRATORY INFECTION

COPD **28**

PHYSICAL RESPIRATORY
OBSTRUCTION *eg* POLYPS **32**

PULMONARY
HAEMORRHAGE **33**

HEART PROBLEM → HEART MURMUR
(p.167)

ATRIAL FIBRILLATION **61**

HEART ARRHYTHMIA
(p.168)

MUSCLE PROBLEM → AZOTURIA **24**

OVER-TRAINED

Modern studwork is an attempt to eliminate failure, but some mares are still hard to get in foal

Difficult to get in foal – what to do

Some mares are difficult to get in foal: the timing of ovulation within the heat period may be abnormal; they may be too old (their fertility is too low); they may have growths/cysts on the ovaries; they may consistently succumb to uterine infection, generally because their vulva is a poor shape (long or sloping). In the latter case, artificial insemination may be a more successful route to take, as it might be for an older mare with a tight cervix. The so-called 'Caslick' operation (in which the upper parts of the vulva lips are stitched together) may help mares with a poorly shaped vulva, as this assists in eliminating the risk of infection.

ULTRASOUND SCAN POSITIVE AT 17–21 DAYS (p.148)

Scanning for pregnancy

ULTRASOUND SCAN NEGATIVE AT 17–21 DAYS (p.148)

SINGLE
FOETUS SEEN → PREGNANCY TEST
AT **42+** DAYS
(POSSIBLY RECTAL,
OR BLOOD TEST)

POSITIVE: MAY
NEED A FURTHER
TEST JUST BEFORE
OCT 1ST IF STUD
PAYMENT RELIES
ON THIS

NEGATIVE: IF SEEN
IN SEASON, SERVE
AGAIN; IF NOT
SEEN IN SEASON,
CONSIDER
HORMONE
TREATMENT

TWINS
DIAGNOSED

LEAVE ALONE

VET ATTEMPTS TO
ABORT JUST ONE
FOETUS

IF CYCLING, SERVE AGAIN

IF NOT CYCLING, CONSIDER
PROSTAGLANDIN TREATMENT
(p.186)

RESTLESS, RAISED TEMPERATURE
(p.155)

FOAL DULL, WITH RAISED
HEART AND RESPIRATORY RATE
(p.178)

STOPS SUCKLING

The importance of colostrum

Make sure the new-born foal has had its first drink
from the mare: this first milk produced by the mare
that has just foaled is called colostrum, and it is
essential to the well-being of the new-born foal
because it contains antibodies that
are readily absorbed across the
small intestine into the
bloodstream, and will destroy
germs – bacteria and viruses – that
would otherwise seriously
compromise the health of the foal.
If a foal does not receive sufficient
colostrum, although he will
probably survive, he can be 50 per
cent more prone to infection for
the rest of his life.

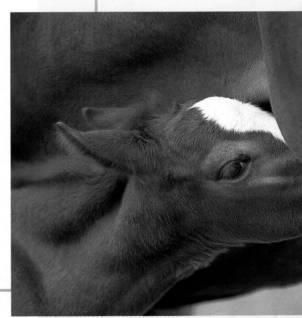

BLIND, BECOMES COMATOSE AND DEHYDRATED (p.157) ⟶ BARKER FOAL **66**

NORMAL SIGHT ⟶ SEPTICAEMIA *eg* SLEEPY FOAL DISEASE **67**

JOINT ILL **68**

SWEATING, ABDOMINAL PAIN ⟶ RETAINED MECONIUM **69**

RUPTURED BLADDER **70**

PALE OR JAUNDICED MEMBRANES IN FIRST FEW DAYS OF LIFE (p.180) ⟶ HAEMOLYTIC ANAEMIA **71**

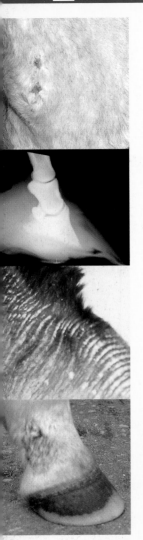

When a word appears in **bold** type in an entry in this section, the reader can refer to Part 3, where the subject is explained more fully; see index to Part 3 on pp.134–5.

Treatments Investigated

1 Ear mites

What to look for

Horses occasionally have problems with a number of skin mites, including the psoroptes species. The horse rubs the affected ear, which may look droopy and have a waxy discharge. An auroscope is needed to look down the ear, but a horse will usually have to be sedated to do this.

How is it treated?

Treatment will involve twice daily applications of parasiticidal drops for a minimum of 7 days.

2 Ear infections

What to look for

Bacterial infections of the ear are rare in the horse. When they do occur they follow an earlier irritant such as ear mites. Gravity tends to keep the resulting **pus** deep down in the ear canal, but if the horse shakes its head then at least some of the pus will become visible on the ear itself.

How is it treated?

Treatment consists of twice daily applications of antibiotic drops such as fucidic acid or neomycin for either 7 days or until 2–3 days after all evidence of infection has disappeared, whichever is the longer.

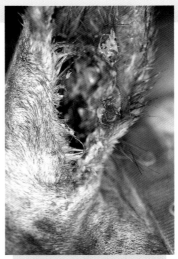

Pus clearly visible on the inside of a horse's ear

3 Dental problems

Congenital problems

Some dental problems are congenital. In a condition known as parrot mouth the upper jaw is longer than the lower jaw, and the incisor teeth at the front of both jaws do not meet. Such a horse cannot graze properly, leading to difficulties in obtaining adequate nutrition if out at grass. However, they can chew hay and concentrate food, and so can compensate for their deformity if the standard of stable management is good enough.

A horse is said to be overshot if the upper incisors are slightly in front of the lower incisors but still in contact with them. It is undershot if the lower incisors protrude in front of the upper ones. These two faults rarely cause dental problems.

Many horses develop sharp points on their molar or cheek teeth. These usually form on the outside edge of the upper teeth or the inside edge of the lower teeth, as a result of wear from the narrower lower jaw on the wider upper jaw. They can occur at any age. Symptoms include resentment of the bit (because the tack presses the cheeks against the sharp edges), allowing incompletely chewed food to drop back out of the mouth (quidding), loss of condition, or colic due to insufficient chewing of the food. The sharp points are removed by rasping. It is good practice to have a horse's teeth checked for their presence at least once a year. This requires the use of a gag to hold the horse's mouth open sufficiently wide for all the teeth to be individually checked. The more precise the control needed of a horse the more sensitive it is likely to be of such dental problems. Dressage horses may need more frequent dental checks than a horse not in any kind of work.

Parrot mouth. There is no contact between upper and lower incisors

Because a horse's molar teeth are continually being pushed further and further out from the jaw, some dental problems become much more common with age. The line across the top chewing surface of the teeth can develop into a wave pattern rather than a straight line, due to uneven eruption and wear, and this interferes with the normal chewing movements of the jaws. The development of overhanging hooks on the first or the last molar similarly greatly restricts chewing movements. If a tooth is lost for any reason, the opposite tooth on the other jaw

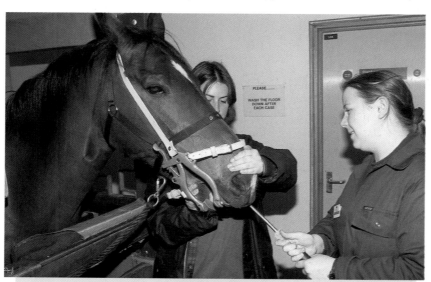
Horse's teeth need to checked regularly. Rasping is necessary to remove any sharp points

65

continues erupting unchecked by wear and can grow into the space left by the lost tooth; this naturally inhibits jaw movement during chewing. All of these situations can cause loss of weight and general unthriftiness unless they are righted. Remedial dentistry of this sort may require the use of power tools or other devices in order to remove the surplus tooth material.

Abscesses

Visible swelling on face due to a build up of pus in the sinus

Tooth root abscesses are particularly serious in horses because in many cases they involve the upper molar teeth whose roots are buried in the large cavities or sinuses that the horse is thought to have developed in an attempt to lighten the weight of the head. Large volumes of **pus** can accumulate before anyone notices the first symptom, which is usually a pusy nasal discharge. **Antibiotics** alone will not solve the problem because the pus still sits in the sinus even if most of the **bacteria** have been killed. Thus the tooth root involved has to be removed to allow proper drainage via the socket, and this is physically quite difficult; so the horse will need a general anaesthetic. There are two ways of approaching the problem. A hole can be drilled through the skull into the sinus and a form of chisel can then be placed against the tooth root and hit with a mallet to repulse the tooth. Alternatively the bone of the upper jaw alongside the tooth can be removed, allowing access to the tooth for its removal laterally.

Incisor teeth can become abnormally worn as a result of a vice called crib-biting; collars are available to help prevent this problem.

Wolf teeth

Wolf teeth are very small molar teeth immediately in front of the permanent molar teeth. They appear at around 3–4 years old. They are too small to play any part in chewing, but because they lack a proper root they are relatively mobile with pressure. Some horses find this movement, which occurs when the bit presses against the wolf tooth, very unpleasant, and will throw their head around in an attempt to move the bit. Wolf teeth can be removed relatively easily in the conscious horse. Again the general rule is that the more precise the control that you need of your horse, the more advantage you are likely to receive from having wolf teeth removed. Sometimes the teeth are incompletely removed, leaving a fractured tooth root behind that works its way to the gum surface much later and causes renewed problems.

Neuralgia

4

Neuralgia is pain in the nerve itself rather than a pain sensation detected in other tissues and transmitted by the nerve. Neuralgia of one of the facial nerves is thought to be one of the causes of head shaking. Neuralgia does not usually respond well to normal painkillers.

Guttural pouch problems

The guttural pouch is a widened section of the eustachian tube that links the inner ear with the pharynx at the back of the mouth. It is almost unique to horses. An endoscope passed through one of the nostrils can be used to examine the inside of the pouch.

Pus can accumulate in the guttural pouch, usually secondary to infection in the surrounding tissues, or in the lymph nodes nearby. The result is a large swelling that can be seen just below the ear. It may be mistaken for a swollen lymph gland or a **tumour**. If the swelling is large it may obstruct the airway and so interfere with breathing; it can also interfere with swallowing. An x-ray may show the level of pus in the pouch. As long as drainage can take place from the pouch's normal entrance there will also be a foul-smelling nasal discharge. Treatment consists of flushing out the pus using a catheter, but sometimes the pus is semisolid and cannot be flushed out. In these cases it may require surgical removal.

A number of important blood vessels such as the internal carotid artery run across the roof of the guttural pouch. The walls of these vessels can become damaged, possibly by a **fungus**. The first indication of the problem is bleeding from a nostril. This can occur at any time ie not just after exercise. The **haemorrhage** may stop, only to return days or weeks later. Haemorrhage can be so great if it involves an artery that it causes death. Treatment with fungicides or with pure oxygen may kill the fungus, but once the wall of an artery has been damaged the vessel may need to be tied off surgically to stop any blood passing along it at all.

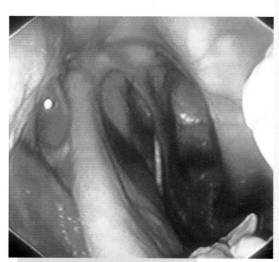

Lumps of dry yellow pus (seen at the bottom of the picture), typically associated with guttural pouch problems

67

6 Insect hypersensitivity

What to look for

Horses can become hypersensitive to the saliva left behind after being bitten by flying insects. The result is a raised lump in the skin at the site of the bite. There can be hundreds of these all over the body, sometimes oozing a small drop of **serum**. The area may be swollen and causing obvious irritation.

How is it treated?

Treatment consists of anti-inflammatories and/or **steroids** to reduce the **hypersensitivity** reaction, but prevention by stabling and the use of insect repellents is vital. See also sweet itch.

7 Laminitis

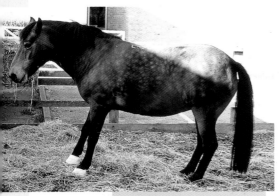

Characteristic laminitic stance

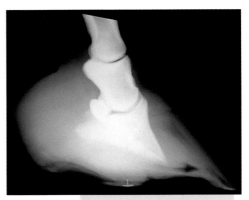

Rotated pedal bone

What is it?

Laminitis literally means inflammation of the sensitive laminae that lie between the hoof and the pedal bone. The basic problem is a lack of oxygen reaching the tissues, but this in turn is caused by a decreased blood supply to the structures of the foot. What happens is that various substances in the blood can cause constriction of small blood vessels, and the laminae are supplied by a network of narrow vessels that start as tiny arteries bringing blood into the foot, gradually becoming veins draining the blood from the foot. Where the sensitive tissues are only a few cells thick there is no alternative blood supply, and when the vessels constrict the tissues start to die. The changes are very painful for the horse and usually affect all four feet, though because the horse takes more weight on its front feet than on the hind ones, the front feet show symptoms more readily.

If sufficient of the laminar tissue is destroyed, the pedal bone will no longer be attached to the inside of the hoof wall and will rotate within the hoof, so that its sharp point is now pressing down towards the sole. In other cases the whole pedal bone sinks down because there is no longer enough living laminar tissue to hold it up against the hoof wall.

The commonest cause of laminitis is a high sugar intake, eg from rich grass; this causes the stomach wall to release **endotoxins** that ultimately cause the blood vessel contraction. Acute infections and problems after foaling are other situations where such endotoxins can be released. Some ponies especially appear to be particularly susceptible to laminitis, although this may be because the laminae do not always completely recover between bouts. Laminitis can also occur for physical reasons, such as excessive weight bearing on a particular foot, or where a localised hoof abscess has weakened the laminar attachment.

Laminitis starts as an apparent stiffness, with the horse unwilling to walk: it tends to lean back on its heels, and may be unwilling to pick up one or more feet because of the pain from taking extra weight on the other feet. The hooves may feel warm to the touch. Because it takes more effort to push blood around the coronet and back up the leg rather than through the normal blood vessels in the feet, an increased **pulse** can often be felt on either side of the pastern in clinical cases. This is a very valuable diagnostic aid that all horse owners should be able to utilise. The horse may also lie down more and be unwilling to stand.

Treatment has two aims. Firstly we try to increase the blood supply to the laminae by dilating the blood vessels using either acetylpromazine or clenbuterol given by mouth. Secondly we provide support via the frog for the pedal bone in an attempt to stop it rotating or sinking. Heart-bar shoes or rubber **frog pad**s can be used for this. Proper trimming of the feet is essential in all cases. Sand is the best bedding for laminitis cases; deep-litter shavings are often used nowadays. Pain killers are necessary, often at high doses. Horses that get recurrent laminitis on lush pastures may benefit from oral virginiamycin, which appears to reduce the amount of endotoxins produced. Complete box rest is essential. The forced exercise that in the past was prescribed for laminitis cases is completely misguided, because in fact it weakens the attachment of the laminae even more.

The prognosis with acute laminitis is always guarded, especially if x-rays show pedal bone rotation, and full recovery may take many months. Furthermore, just because the horse becomes sound, it does not mean that the laminae have recovered completely.

Lymphosarcoma 8

A lymphosarcoma is a particularly malignant type of **tumour**. In the horse it most commonly affects the gut walls, and because these can no longer absorb nutrients properly the horse loses weight. This weight loss can be quite rapid because the tumour spreads so quickly. The horse may develop diarrhoea because the intestines can no longer reabsorb fluid.

No treatment is possible and **euthanasia** may be required.

9 Epiglottic entrapment

What is it? The epiglottis is a cartilaginous flap whose role is to cover the entrance to the larynx when the horse swallows, thus preventing food going down the trachea, or windpipe, rather than down the oesophagus. Inflammation and swelling of the folds of membrane that link the epiglottis to the larynx trap the epiglottis under a layer of membrane.

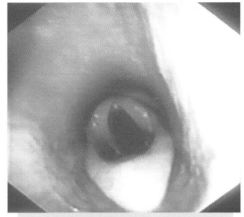

The pink V-shaped fold of membrane at the bottom of the picture covers the epiglottis, causing entrapment

What to look for The horse makes an abnormal noise when breathing at exercise. It may also cough and choke at rest. Some horses on the other hand do not appear to be inconvenienced by the condition at all, and in other horses the condition only occurs intermittently anyway.

How is it treated? Surgery can release the epiglottis.

10 Laryngeal hemiplegia

What is it? At the entrance to the horse's larynx are two folds of membrane called the vocal cords. Muscles either pull them to the side when a maximum airway is needed during strenuous exercise, or they relax and allow them to fall back almost across the airway at rest. Degeneration of the left recurrent laryngeal nerve in the neck will result in paralysis of the left vocal cord (the right cord is only extremely rarely affected). Sometimes there may be a hereditary predisposition to the condition. Viral infections or

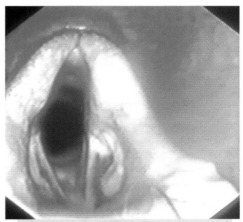

The paralysed vocal cord (on the right when viewed from the front) is almost vertical in stature

trauma can also damage the nerve. This means that a horse can develop the condition at any stage in its life, and this is significant when a horse is purchased because in turn it means that a thorough examination may reveal nothing, but the horse may still develop laryngeal hemiplegia later.

Because the relaxed vocal cord partially obstructs the airway and causes turbulence in the airflow, the horse will make a characteristic **roaring** noise when breathing in during fast work, and its exercise tolerance is reduced because of the reduced oxygen supply to the lungs. A roaring noise when the horse breathes out is not a symptom of laryngeal hemiplegia, only a noise on inspiration.

Having confirmed the diagnosis by endoscopic examination, a decision has to be made as to whether it actually interferes with performance rather than just causes a noise. A Hobday operation reduces the air turbulence by removing two membranous sacs behind the vocal cords, but it does not improve the airway. A laryngeal prosthesis operation pulls the vocal cord to the side and holds it there permanently. This does increase the airway, but there is a slight danger that food particles may get into the larynx in the absence of this normal safety system, causing a chronic cough.

How is it treated?

Atheroma 11

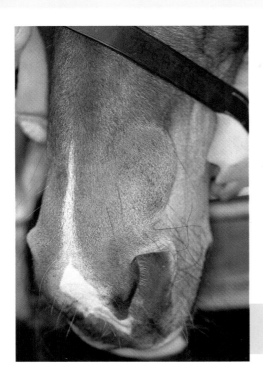

The swelling above the nostril is very obvious, but painless

An atheroma is a localised **benign tumour** under the skin of the false nostril. It causes a swelling by the nostril but does not usually have a significant effect on breathing.

What is it?

The atheroma can be removed surgically.

How is it treated?

71

12 Collapsed nostril

What is it? Small muscles on the muzzle control the size of the horse's nostril, dilating it greatly when there is maximum demand for air during strenuous exercise. Damage to or paralysis of these muscles leaves the nostril flaccid and unresponsive to increased oxygen demand. The floppy rim of the nostril vibrates in such circumstances, causing an abnormal noise on both breathing in and breathing out. As the nostrils are not the narrowest part of the airway the condition does not usually reduce performance.

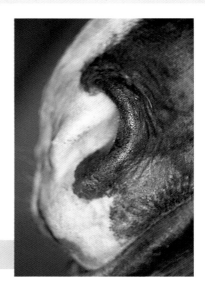

The horse's airway is blocked by the upper fleshy nostril

13 Dorsal displacement of the soft palate

What is it? Dorsal displacement of the soft palate is really a situation where the larynx is pulled ventrally by the neck muscles during an extreme need for air rather than a movement of the soft palate itself. The epiglottis and larynx no longer protrude through the space in the soft palate, and the soft palate itself acts like a valve that is sucked across the entrance to the larynx.

The larynx is almost below the level of the soft palate

What to look for An affected horse suddenly makes loud gurgling noises during strenuous exercise and pulls itself up because of the lack of air. It is thus self-curing because as the horse then relaxes the larynx resumes its normal position with the epiglottis hooked over the soft palate. The horse can then breathe normally again. The condition is sometimes called tongue swallowing.

How is it treated? Tying the tongue tightly to the lower jaw in such a way as to prevent the tongue being pulled backwards may help prevent the displacement occurring. A **bitless bridle** may enable the horse to hold its head in such a way as to prevent the displacement occurring. Surgery that cuts the muscles that pull on the larynx, and allowing them to heal lengthened by a section of scar tissue so that they cannot pull so tightly, has also been successful.

Insect bites

14

Horses are bitten by a variety of insects, especially whilst out grazing. So-called 'horse flies' can produce either a definite raised lump or a larger area of oedema at the site of the bite. No treatment is usually needed as the lumps go down quite quickly.

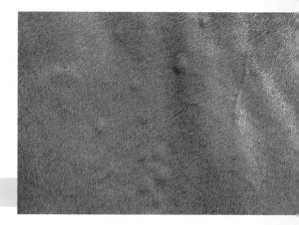

Bites will often occur in large numbers, as seen here

Abscesses

15

An abscess is a localised collection of **pus** at a focus of infection. Abscesses are usually warm to the touch and painful. They increase in size as the amount of pus increases, and usually eventually rupture through the overlying tissues such as the skin due to the pressure of the amount of pus forming.

What is it?

Abscesses can occur anywhere (including internally). Because the horse absorbs toxins from the abscess it may well have a raised temperature and be lethargic, and not be eating very well.

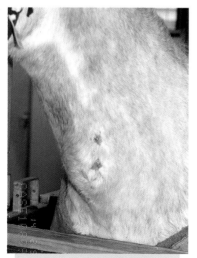

An abscess at the base of the neck

Rupture of an abscess can bring about an almost instant relief from the pain as the pressure is relieved. Unfortunately they often rupture near the top of the accumulated pus rather than at the bottom, and so the pus never completely drains out. The abscess may then seal over temporarily, only to break out again at either the same or a different place later.

The principles of dealing with an abscess are to ensure free drainage of all the pus, flushing it out if necessary. Local or systemic treatment with **antibiotics** can then be used to kill the infection. It is important that a burst or lanced abscess does not seal over before all the infection has been killed.

How is it treated?

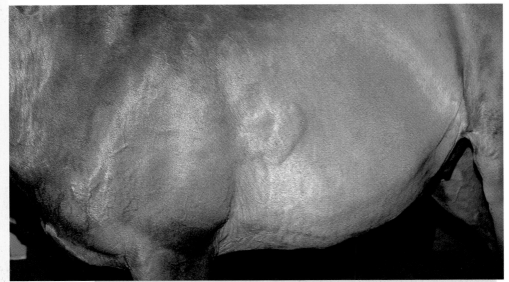

A haematoma clearly visible on the chest wall

What is it?

A haematoma is the equivalent of a large blood blister, being a localised collection of blood from a damaged blood vessel. The blood does not clot at first because it is inside rather than outside the body. If the blood is drained off the haematoma will reform until the blood vessel break has healed itself. The brisket is probably the commonest site for haematomas in the horse.

What to look for

It is important to differentiate between a haematoma and an abscess. The former is soft and obviously fluid-filled from the start, rather than hard becoming soft as the abscess prepares to burst. Unlike an abscess a haematoma is not warm to the touch, and is painless.

How is it treated?

Drainage of a haematoma must be done in such a way that it is impossible for the openings to seal before the **haemorrhage** has completely stopped, and there is a variety of techniques for ensuring this. Left alone the body does eventually reabsorb the fluid, leaving the blood cells incorporated in a form of clot. This may cause some distortion of surrounding tissues. Haematomas can become infected at a later date and then turn into an abscess.

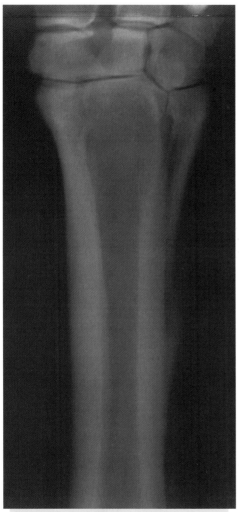

Splints form as a response to weak bone being stressed. New bone can be seen here on the right, around the narrow splint bone. Despite the initial discomfort, they settle down and can decrease in size or disappear completely

What is it?

Each leg of the horse has two splint bones, one on either side of the cannon bone. However, when we talk about splints we are referring to an area of new bone that forms on the ligament holding the splint bone against the cannon bone. Splints form in response to stress on relatively weak bone. Because the inside of the leg takes more of the weight than the outside, splints will usually form on the inside of the cannon bone.

What to look for

Most splints cause no clinical symptoms at all; they can appear literally overnight and never alter in size. On the other hand they can develop slowly, with the horse lame even before there is anything to see or feel; but even when splints are initially painful they usually settle down after 2–3 weeks. They will sometimes decrease in size over 4–6 weeks as an initially fibrous swelling consolidates into a smaller area of actual bone. Sometimes they disappear altogether after a year or two.

How is it treated?

If a splint is causing lameness, a marked decrease in exercise levels is needed to allow the new bone to mature without further stress. Occasionally the splint remains painful and the bone remains active. In such cases it is worth x-raying to make sure there are no complications such as a fracture of the splint bone itself. Applying cold compresses to the area or cold hosing it may reduce the inflammation, as may topical applications such as DMSO. Pulsed magnetic therapy may be of value. If lameness persists, it is advisable to turn the horse away and rest him for at least two months.

18 Sarcoids

What is it? Sarcoids are a particular type of skin **tumour**. They are probably caused by the transmission of the **cancer** cells from one horse to another, or from one place to another on a particular horse. A horse may have just one sarcoid, or it may have a couple of dozen scattered over the body. They may grow only slowly over the years, or they may suddenly increase either in size, or in the amount of inflammation or ulceration associated with them. Sarcoids commonly occur in sites of friction such as the girth area. They can become ulcerated and infected.

How is it treated? Sarcoids do not disappear on their own. If they are removed surgically, then at least 50 per cent of them will return. Injecting BCG vaccine into a sarcoid may stimulate enough local reaction to cause an immune response that destroys the tumour. Heavy metals applied as an ointment can have the same effect. 5 per cent thiouracil cream is less effective but readily available. When sarcoids are close to a sensitive structure such as the eye, a form of irradiation therapy may be required to destroy the tumour.

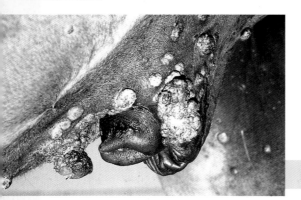

Multiple small sarcoids around a horse's sheath

19 Melanoma

What is it? A melanoma is a **tumour** of the cells that manufacture the black pigment called melanin. Because grey horses have more of these cells in their skin than other coat colours, melanomas are more common in greys. Melanomas are also more common in older horses, under the tail or around the rectum.

Skin melanomas hardly ever cause any problems other than a cosmetic one, but melanomas can also occur internally where they can be more troublesome.

A group of melanomas around the throat area

An infected horn will be black in colour and around the cleft of the frog

Thrush is an infection of the horn of the hoof, including the frog. The horn matrix becomes softened by moisture, often aggravated by ammonia compounds in wet bedding. A **bacterial** infection invades and further softens the horn, and this produces a foul-smelling black substance. The cleft between frog and hoof is a common site to find this. As the infection reaches the deeper sensitive structures of the foot the horse becomes lame.

Treatment starts with providing a dry environment. Then all the infected horn has to be cut away. Antibiotic/antiseptic dressing applied to the horn will kill any remaining infection. Diluted formalin solution is a very effective traditional remedy, although care must be taken not to breathe in its fumes.

Biotin & DL methionine deficiencies 21

Both biotin and DL methionine are vitamin-like substances that the horse needs in its diet. They are both essential to form the chemical sulphur bonds that hold the tubules of horn firm in the hoof. A deficiency of either substance results in weak bonds, and so poor quality horn. The hooves crack at the edges and break away easily. The horn may also be less resistant to infections.

It may be more accurate to say that some horses have a higher requirement for these substances than to say that they are receiving less than the 'average' horse requires. It is customary to include both substances in any supplement aimed to help hoof quality, although some of the cheaper supplements may not provide significant amounts.

22 Anhydrosis

What is it?
Anhydrosis is the failure of the horse's sweating mechanism: it is usually the result of exhaustion of the sweat glands in the skin. The skin itself becomes dry and scurfy. The horse is lethargic and takes very much longer than normal to recover from exercise because its heat regulatory system has lost its major way of cooling the body.

How is it treated?
Anhydrosis often occurs due to a failure to acclimatise to a different part of the world. There is no treatment other than resting the horse and keeping it cool in the hope that the glands will recover. Unfortunately the majority of affected horses do not return to normal. **Shampooing** so as to remove the scurf, especially using a benzoyl peroxide shampoo, may improve the coat quality.

23 Horner's syndrome

What is it?
Damage to the sympathetic nerve supply to the eyeball causes the pupil to constrict slightly, and the third eyelid, or nictitating membrane, to become more visible. The ear may not be held erect. Areas of sweating can occur anywhere on the face and neck. The function of the eye is not affected.

How is it caused?
Causes might include damage or a blow to the neck, perhaps in a fall, an infection of the guttural pouch, tumours, or surgery in the carotid artery/vagus nerve area.

How is it treated?
No treatment is possible. The condition may be temporary or permanent – this will depend on the cause.

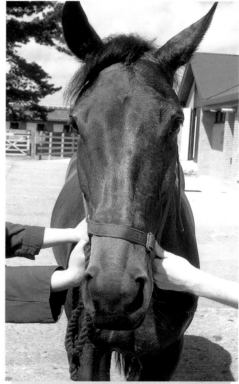

A horse suffering from Horner's syndrome, with one ear hanging lower than the other

This condition is known by a number of names, including exertional rhabdomyelitis and set-fast. It is basically a problem in the way that the muscles deal with glycogen, a starch used as an energy store. When glycogen is broken down to release energy in the absence of oxygen (anaerobic metabolism), then lactic acid is formed. If either large quantities are formed, or if the acid is not removed quickly enough by the bloodstream, then the acid damages the muscle fibres. The susceptibility of those muscle fibres to damage can also depend on the levels of sodium, calcium and chloride that the individual horse has in its tissues, because these affect the stability of the muscle cell wall.

Traditionally azoturia was associated with overfeeding a resting horse with high energy feeds (which resulted in large amounts of glycogen being stored in the muscles, especially the big muscle masses of the back and the hindquarters). A return to work, and so a sudden demand for energy, results in rapid anaerobic metabolism of the glycogen and the release of large amounts of lactic acid. However, the problem can occur in many other scenarios because of the number of metabolic factors involved in stabilising the muscle cell walls.

The main symptom of azoturia is muscle pain, but this can vary in severity from a slight decrease in athletic performance to the horse becoming recumbent, with its major muscles hard, sweating and painful. A blood sample will confirm the diagnosis by detecting high levels of the enzymes *creatine phosphokinase* and *aspartate transferase* from the damaged muscle cells. Affected horses may have difficulty passing urine, and the urine may be very dark in colour as the filtering system of the kidneys becomes clogged by muscle breakdown products. Any horse that sweats more than expected during exercise, or which has reduced exercise tolerance, should raise suspicions of azoturia.

Treatment consists of complete rest. In acute cases horses should not be moved at all, even by horse transport. The horse should be on a low **carbohydrate** diet. Anti-inflammatories will help with the pain, and **diuretics** such as frusemide help the kidneys to eliminate the muscle breakdown products. Vitamin E supplements may help muscle recovery. Electrolyte supplementation may be valuable, and all cases will probably benefit from at least 1oz of salt per day to help stabilise the muscle cell membranes.

Depending on the existence of any underlying causes, most horses recover eventually, but normal work should not be resumed until the muscle enzyme levels have completely returned to normal.

25 Colic

What is it? The term 'colic' means abdominal pain. That pain can be due to a variety of causes, and the different types of colic diagnosed are based on both the cause of the pain and/or the part of the intestinal tract involved. The pain causes the horse to look around at its belly or to kick at it. If the pain is dull but constant the horse may lie on its side or back almost completely motionless. Acute spasms of pain may

A horse rolling violently on the ground is a typical indication of colic

stimulate the horse to roll violently on the ground. Sweating is common. An increased **pulse** rate above 60 per minute may be the result of pain, but more seriously it may reflect major blood circulation problems. A **capillary refill time** of over 4 seconds is a worrying sign. Vets may carry out a **rectal examination** in order to obtain further information, especially about the position of the various sections of the intestines. Owners should never attempt to do this because the bowel wall is very easily ruptured, with possibly fatal results.

A Spasmodic colic

What is it? This refers to pain that is present for perhaps 20–30 minutes but then disappears, only to return again later. It is probably the commonest type of colic and is often caused by disturbance of the nervous system to the intestines eg by the horse being frightened. The pain is caused solely by abnormal gut motility, and treatment consists of antispasmodics such as a hyoscine/dipyrone mixture to restore normal bowel movements. Walking the horse in hand does not treat colic: it may distract the horse sufficiently to prevent it rolling, but if the horse still rolls outside the stable, the wounds it inflicts on itself may be considerable. Prolonged walking also tires the horse at a time when its circulation is already under pressure.

B Tympanitic colic

What is it? This refers to the presence of a large quantity of gas, the pressure from which causes the pain. It is a serious type of colic because so often there is a sinister reason as to why that gas cannot pass along the digestive tract and escape. Gastric tympany and caecal tympany can be associated with particularly violent and acute symptoms.

Relief will only be obtained by relieving the gas pressure, and to do this the horse may require surgery.

How is it treated?

Impactions C

Why does it occur?

Impactions, as the name implies, occur when the intestinal contents cease to move along the intestine. This is most commonly associated with the contents being poorly digested or fibrous. A particularly common site for this to occur is in the large colon, which at one point bends through 180° and decreases rapidly in diameter. Tapeworms living at the junction between the small intestine and the caecum may trigger off an impaction.

How is it treated?

Large quantities of liquid paraffin, perhaps 5l at a time, given by stomach pump, may soften and lubricate the impaction, and result in it passing along the intestine; but surgical removal may be necessary. Because the impaction may develop gradually, the symptoms may also develop over a period of several days. The earlier treatment is commenced, the better the chance of treating the impaction medically rather than surgically.

What to look for

If a horse becomes quieter than normal, eating less or not at all, and lying down more often than normal, then an impaction should be considered a possibility. A horse will still pass faeces for several days after an impaction has formed, so the presence of droppings does not rule out the possibility of an impaction.

Twisted gut D

Displacement of one or more parts of the intestines is the true 'twisted gut' that used to be diagnosed for any fatal colic in the days before surgery became a feasible proposition to investigate serious colics. Lengths of intestine can become twisted on themselves, but can also become trapped in another loop of intestine or around other abdominal structures. Surgery is the only hope in the treatment of these displacements, and the sooner it is carried out the better, as the affected length of intestine may start to die.

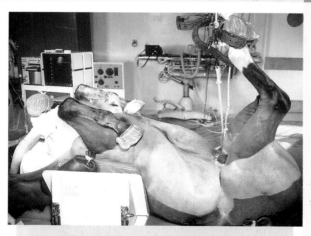

Surgery is the only option for serious displacements of the intestine, as in twisted gut

26 | Grass sickness

What is it?

Grass sickness is one of the real mysteries of the horse. Originally only found in Scotland, it has now spread to the rest of the UK and to other countries. Although the precise cause of the disease is still unknown, some toxic damage occurs in the nervous system, especially that supplying the digestive tract. A definitive diagnosis can only be made by finding characteristic microscopic changes in the nerves along the intestine. Despite the uncertainty as to the cause of grass sickness, we do know that certain fields have a higher incidence of the disease, and cases often occur after horses have been grazing in cold, wet spring conditions.

What to look for

Chronic grass sickness causes weight loss over a number of weeks. Some horses recover naturally from this form of the disease. More acutely all bowel movement ceases. The stomach becomes full of greenish fluid, but the rest of the intestinal contents become hard and dry. The horse is unable to swallow, and it may stand drooling over its water. Muscle twitching can often be seen, especially over the neck and shoulders.

How is it treated?

There is no cure for grass sickness. In less acute cases cisapride can be used to maintain bowel movement, and this may keep the horse alive long enough for it to overcome the disease itself. However, acute cases are almost invariably fatal, and as such are euthanased once the diagnosis is certain.

27 | Choke

What is it?

Food should pass quickly down the oesophagus into the stomach. If dry food swells up rapidly on contact with saliva, it may become stuck in the oesophagus. A similar situation sometimes occurs when a horse eats some dry food too quickly and in the absence of saliva it sticks to the moist oesophageal lining.

Frothy discharge from both nostrils of a horse with choke

How is it treated?

The horse becomes very distressed. Saliva may dribble out of the mouth, and froth may appear at the nostrils. It may be possible to see the obstruction as a swelling on the lower left side of the neck. Smooth muscle relaxant drugs may allow the food to pass on, but in many cases the obstruction has to be flushed away slowly but surely via a **stomach tube**.

As the name implies, this involves constriction of the small airways, or bronchioles, in the lungs, thus obstructing the air flow to the air sacs, or alveoli, where oxygen transfer to the blood takes place. Because the horse breathing in (inspiration) involves a muscular effort by the chest, but breathing out (expiration) is a passive movement, affected horses can breathe in satisfactorily despite the obstruction. Expiration, however, is often broken into two stages: normal passive expiration, and then a separate muscular effort to empty the lungs. The latter is necessary because passive expiration against the obstruction is only partially successful. This double-stage expiration is responsible for the name 'broken wind'.

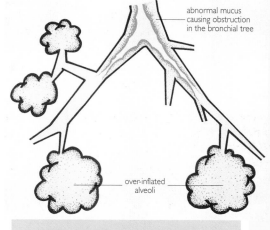

abnormal mucus causing obstruction in the bronchial tree

over-inflated alveoli

An allergic reaction will cause abnormal mucus in the lungs

Most cases of COPD are reversible, and once the airways return to normal then the horse performs normally again. Very occasionally breathing in forcibly without proper emptying of the lungs results in over-inflation and rupture of the air sacs, a condition that is called emphysema. The cause of the bronchiolar obstruction is usually an allergic reaction that causes contraction of the smooth muscle fibres in the bronchiolar wall. Horses that develop COPD whilst stabled have usually become hypersensitive to the fungal spores found on hay and bedding; these do not have to be visibly mouldy for there to be very large numbers of such spores present. Horses that first develop COPD at pasture have usually become hypersensitive to specific types of pollen – and once a horse becomes hypersensitive it will remain so for the rest of its life.

Mouldy forage. Mould will not necessarily be visible if there are large numbers of spores present

The main symptom of COPD is a chronic cough; there may also be a nasal discharge, and the **respiratory rate** is increased. The horse's exercise tolerance is decreased. The broken expiration may be visible, and chronically affected horses develop a so-called 'heave line' on their abdominal wall as the muscles used in the forced expiration enlarge with use.

Removing the cause of the **allergy** will usually result in the airways returning to normal, although the longer the horse has been coughing, the longer this will take. It has been suggested that it will take 50 per cent longer for the bronchiolar walls to relax than it took for the allergic constriction to develop in the first place: so if stabling an affected horse for 4 weeks has produced symptoms, it will take 6 weeks at pasture for the situation to return to normal. Stabled horses should be turned out to grass, or stabled on shavings and fed a hay-free diet in a stable with no airspace shared with hay or straw. Clenbuterol is a smooth-muscle relaxant that opens up the bronchioles and restores them to normal more quickly. Because of the similarity of COPD to human asthma, a number of asthma nebuliser treatments have also been used in horses over the years.

29 Congestive heart failure

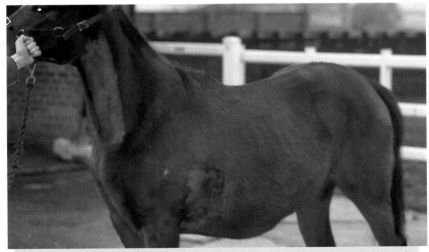

Swelling underneath the body due to oedema associated with a heart problem

Anything that interferes with the pumping ability of the heart can result in congestive heart failure, so both **heart murmurs** and **arrhythmias** may be involved. The heart output is decreased, but the cardiac return is not, so there is an increasing amount of blood being held up in the lungs waiting to be pumped around the body again. In such circumstances fluid will leak out through the blood vessel walls into the surrounding lung tissue – hence the lung congestion. Modern **ultrasound** doppler scans can measure how much blood is being pumped out by the heart, which is important both for diagnosis and for assessing the consequent effects of treatment.

The horse can put up with a surprising amount of congestive heart failure before clinical signs appear. These symptoms always involve exercise intolerance and the horse may have a chronic cough. In severe cases it will become lethargic and may collapse.

What to look for

Treatment depends on the cause of the decreased heart performance. The diuretic frusemide can help reduce existing congestion but horses may need to be retired from active work.

How is it treated?

Pneumonia 30

What is it?

Conditions that cause inflammation of the lung tissue are referred to as pneumonia. The cause may be an infection. Foals are very susceptible to pneumonia caused by an infection with the bacterium *Rhodococcus equi*. It causes numerous small abscesses scattered through the lungs. Horses of any age can suffer from inhalation pneumonia caused by solid or liquid material being sucked down into the lung alveoli. Milk can do down 'the wrong way' into the lungs when a foal suckles its mother or, more commonly, a bottle. Such foreign material then acts as an irritant causing a tremendous inflammatory reaction. Even inhalation pneumonias can often become infected secondarily.

The inhalation of milk while suckling can cause a foal to develop pneumonia

There are a number of factors that make pneumonia difficult to treat. Gravity tends to keep any fluid produced down in the lungs. Only if the horse spends time with its head right down near the floor can such material drain out naturally. Lung tissue has a very good blood supply of course, and this helps infections firstly to multiply and then to spread rapidly into the bloodstream.

What to look for

Coughing does not always occur in pneumonia. The horse will always have some interference with its breathing. The **respiratory rate** is increased, often to the extent that the respiratory rate equals the heart rate (rather than being in the ratio of 1:3 as it usually is). There may be a nasal discharge. In inhalation pneumonia especially this can be foul smelling and coloured.

How is it treated?

Antibiotic therapy to treat the condition needs to be at a high dosage to help the penetration of the drug into the inflamed lungs, and needs to be continued until all the inflammation has resolved.

31 Acute hypersensitivity

Why does it occur?

A **hypersensitivity** or **allergy** to something usually stimulates just a local reaction, but occasionally the whole body reacts.

What to look for

One of the more dramatic results of this is that the small bronchioles in the lungs constrict, causing rapid shallow breathing such as in a very acute form of COPD. The **respiratory rate** is markedly increased. The whole body may develop areas of oedematous swelling.

How is it treated?

Injections of vaccines and other substances can trigger off an acute hypersensitivity reaction that requires emergency treatment with **steroids** and other **anti-inflammatory** agents in order to safeguard the air supply to the lungs.

Hypersensitive reactions might include *urticaria*, a systematic reaction usually due to a sudden change in diet, for example new spring grass; *photosensitivity*, where photosensitive agents build up in skin and increase sensitivity to sunlight; and *nettle rash*, a hypersensitive reaction to nettle stings.

Polyps are **benign tumour**s that are attached to the surface by a distinct narrow neck. They tend to grow just to a certain size limit and then no further, and only rarely cause a threat in themselves.

Nasal polyps occur just inside one of the nostrils. They cause air turbulence during both inspiration and expiration, which results in an abnormal noise during

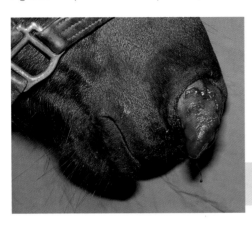

breathing. The larger the polyps are, the more likely they are to interfere with the vital airflow to the lungs.

Fortunately their narrow neck makes the surgical removal of many polyps relatively easy.

Nasal polyps do not necessarily become quite as visible as this one

EIPH (Exercise-induced pulmonary haemorrhage) 33

The majority of racehorses have been shown to have **haemorrhage**d into their lungs after strenuous exercise, and this probably applies to other athletic horses

as well. Only in a relatively low percentage of animals is the amount of haemorrhage so great that blood becomes visible at the nostrils. For a long time this blood was thought to have originated in the nose. Only when **endoscopy** came into general use was it shown that the origin of the haemorrhage was in a particular dorsal lobe of the lungs. It is likely that anything that causes airway obstruction to even a small level can trigger the condition. Racehorses may be particularly prone to it as they are galloped

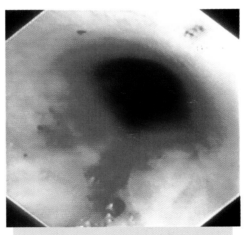

A 'river' of blood can be common along the windpipe as a result of an EIPH

with their head held in a 'collected' position and this restricts the airway between the head and the lungs. Respiratory viral infections are common trigger factors, both because they cause local bronchoconstriction in the lungs, and because they may weaken blood vessels in that particular area of the lung.

There is not necessarily a correlation between the amount of haemorrhage and the chances of blood becoming visible at the nostrils. This makes it unfair that some racing authorities penalise or ban from future races horses that have been seen to have a nose bleed. The effect of bleeding on performance is far from clear.

How is it treated?

Treatment to open the airways in a similar way to that used in COPD may reduce the incidence. In some countries, especially some states of the USA, frusemide is used routinely for any affected horses. It is likely that this acts by having a bronchodilator effect. The use of a **bitless bridle** may allow the horse to adopt a galloping posture that does not restrict the airway. Antibiotic therapy after any respiratory infection may help to remove the low-level **bacterial** infection that so often acts as the trigger factor.

34 Tracheal collapse

What is it?

The trachea, or windpipe, is a flexible round tube that extends from the larynx to the lungs. It is made up of a series of circular cartilage rings that ensure that it maintains a constant circular diameter despite the strong suction forces as the horse breathes in, and the blowing forces as it breathes out.

What to look for

Occasionally the trachea collapses – meaning that the tracheal rings are no longer whole or rigid, and a cross-section across the trachea shows an ellipse rather than a circle. This can be the result of trauma to a localised area of the trachea, but it can also occur in older horses as a result of degenerative changes in the cartilage rings. Whatever the cause, the result is that now when the horse breathes air through the narrowed section of the trachea the breathing is noisy. Because airflow is reduced, exercise tolerance is reduced as well. Sometimes the horse will only show symptoms during hard work, when the suction from the lungs during inspiration pulls the opposite walls of the affected trachea even closer together.

How is it treated?

Surgery is the only form of treatment. A variety of techniques have been used to hold the tracheal wall out in a circular shape, but this has to be done without damaging the tracheal lining membrane, which would otherwise form a scar and even further decrease the airway.

Site of the sinuses

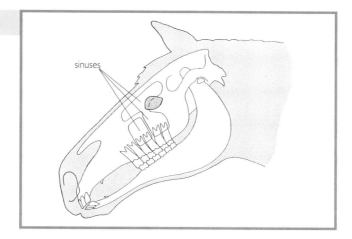

sinuses

The horse's head is quite a heavy structure, but it would be heavier still if it were not for the large air-filled cavities, or sinuses, that lie behind the forehead and down the face. Each of these sinuses has an opening communicating with the nasal chambers or with the pharynx. This allows any mucus formed by the membrane lining the sinus to drain out, and also allows fresh air to enter the sinus. In some cases important structures such as teeth roots protrude into the sinus.

What are the sinuses?

If an infection becomes established in a sinus we face a number of problems in treating the condition. For a start the volume of each sinus is large, and so a large volume of **pus** may accumulate. An x-ray may show the line at the surface of this pus inside the otherwise air-filled sinus. The pus may drain out through the entrance hole, causing a nasal discharge that usually, but not always, only affects one nostril. However, this drainage may become blocked, or the pus may be too thick or dry to pass through the hole, in which case the bony wall of the sinus may start to visibly bulge as pressure builds up. Unfortunately the drainage points are not at the lowest point of the sinus, so complete drainage never occurs anyway. Not surprisingly, in those sinuses containing teeth roots we usually find that these also become infected, making the condition even more painful. Indeed it might be that the infection gains entry to the sinus up a damaged tooth pulp. Affected horses stop eating and may become lethargic as they absorb toxins from the pus.

How is infection treated?

Antibiotic therapy alone is rarely successful in completely eliminating sinus infections. There is, after all, only a small area of contact between the **antibiotics** in the lining membrane and the **bacteria** in the pus that has accumulated. If a tooth root is involved, then that tooth may need to be removed under general anaesthetic. This provides additional drainage as well. In all cases a hole is drilled through the skull into the sinus in order to allow the sinus to be thoroughly flushed out every day. These holes heal over quickly once left alone, and eventually the new bone that seals the sinus is as hard as the original bone.

What is it?

Strangles is an extremely infectious disease caused by a bacterium *Streptococcus equi*. It is most common when young horses are mixed together for the first time, but clinical cases can occur in horses of any age. Some horses may become carriers: they show no symptoms, but have **bacteria** present on the surface of their pharynx at the back of the mouth for very long periods. Localised epidemics of strangles often start as a result of a carrier being introduced into a new group of horses.

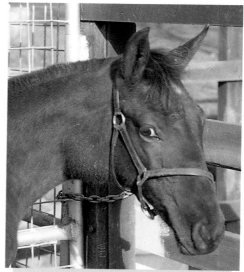

An abscess causing swelling just below the angle of the jaw. They are painful and can burst both internally and externally

What to look for

The bacteria become trapped in the lymph nodes around the horse's jaw and throat. The glands swell tremendously in size as large abscesses form. Abscesses bursting inwards are responsible for thick **pus** appearing at the nostrils, and sometimes the abscesses burst externally through the skin. The horse develops a high temperature. It is a combination of this and physical discomfort from the abscesses around the throat that causes the horse to stop eating. Pressure from abscesses can interfere with normal breathing.

How is it treated?

The streptococcus is usually susceptible to **antibiotics** such as penicillin. Many vets prefer to delay treatment until the abscesses have burst in order to avoid any risk of the bacteria becoming walled off in the glands even after the antibiotic has cleared the rest of the body, but this is not always possible. In some countries vaccines are available, but their use is not without risk. New surface-active vaccines have shown great promise, especially at preventing the development of carriers, but are not yet available commercially. After an outbreak of strangles all the horses on the premises should have naso-pharyngeal swabs cultured in order to detect any carriers, which can then receive further treatment.

The bacteria can become trapped in internal lymph nodes, perhaps as a result of pus being swallowed into the digestive system. The problems caused by such internal abscesses include colic. The condition is known as bastard strangles. *Purpura haemorrhagica* can be a serious sequel to an attack of strangles.

In horses the herpes **viruses**, EHV 1 and EHV 2, mainly cause respiratory problems. In severe cases EHV 1 can cause **abortion** or ataxia, with or without the respiratory symptoms. EHV 4 usually only causes respiratory symptoms.

What is it?

The respiratory signs include coughing and a clear nasal discharge. The **lymph glands** around the throat can be swollen. Just before the appearance of clinical symptoms there may be a raised temperature. The condition is also called rhinopneumonitis.

What to look for

All herpes can have carrier animals and it is the movement of these that triggers off outbreaks of 'the cough' or 'the virus' in stables, or abortion storms at studs. There is no specific treatment. Respiratory symptoms are eased by the use of **bronchodilators** such as clenbuterol. Hygiene and isolation of clinical cases is vital, especially in controlling abortion storms. Vaccines are available, but are not yet completely effective. If horses become paralysed with the neurological form of the disease, high quality nursing will be necessary if the horse is to survive; but even these horses can eventually return to normal work. There is good reason for giving a 10-day course of **antibiotics** to all cases in order to remove the secondary **bacterial** infection that often occurs, and which may in turn lead to future problems such as EIPH.

How is it treated?

COMMON VIRAL DISEASES OF THE HORSE

DISEASE	Special features	CONTROL
Adenovirus	Affects foals	No vaccine
Equine Herpes Virus Type 1	Common everywhere Can also cause abortion	Vaccine reduces abortion
Type 2	No clinical symptoms	No vaccine
Type 3	Usually causes coital exanthema rather than respiratory symptoms	No vaccine
Type 4	Can also cause ataxia and paralysis	No vaccine
Equine influenza Miami, Prague, Kentucky and Suffolk strains	Epidemics common when new strain arises	Vaccine should include strain responsible. Some cross-immunity.
Equine rhinovirus	Common everywhere	No vaccine
African horse sickness	Spread by biting midges. Respiratory symptoms in acute forms	Vaccine needs to include specific strain
Equine viral arteritis	Spread by air droplets and by venereal route	Vaccination possible

38 Equine influenza

What is it?

There are several strains of equine influenza **virus**, (see **bacteria/virus**) divided into two main groups: the type 1 virus was first isolated in Prague in 1956, and the type 2 strain in Miami in 1963. The latter group are the most common. The disease is extremely infectious, and when epidemics occur, they seriously disrupt equine activities such as racing.

What to look for

Infected horses have a dry cough. There is a nasal discharge that may start clear, but becomes thick and purulent. The horse has a temperature of around 103°F. Particularly dangerous are the secondary changes: these might include damage to the heart muscles, and lung damage that may trigger off COPD later. Foals and donkeys are very susceptible to the disease and may die.

How is it treated?

As a viral disease there is no specific treatment, other than using **vaccination** to prevent the disease. A number of different types of vaccine are available, and new intra-nasal vaccines being developed show great promise. It is important that the vaccine used specifically includes the virus strain involved in any outbreak if at all possible. **Bronchodilators** reduce the effects of the infection on the lung, and **antibiotics** are important to prevent secondary infections. Complete rest (for at least 6 weeks in severe cases) is essential.

39 Ethmoid haematoma

What is it?

This is not really a haematoma at all: it is a form of **tumour** involving the ethmoid bone at the back of the nostrils. This bone has a very profuse blood supply, and the blood vessels become eroded. The horse may have a persistent bloody discharge from one of the nostrils, though sooner or later a severe **haemorrhage** occurs. This can be fatal.

How is it treated?

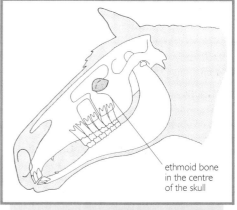

ethmoid bone in the centre of the skull

Site of the ethmoid bone

Endoscopy reveals the large bloody mass in front of the ethmoid bone. Prompt surgery is the only treatment, but it carries a degree of risk because of the substantial volume of blood that is inevitably lost during the removal of the abnormal tissue.

The horse's willingness to respond to the demands of its driver or rider can result in physical exhaustion occurring, usually when the rider is concentrating on success in a competition rather than on the welfare of the horse. Scientifically what happens is that the glycogen and other fuel reserves in the muscles become exhausted. The muscles can no longer contract properly, and even standing requires muscle contraction. The horse will sweat profusely as the body tries to get rid of the heat produced by its muscles. Hot, humid conditions increase the risk of exhaustion by reducing the efficacy of sweating. Loss of calcium in the sweat can cause a form of hiccups called 'asynchronous diaphragmatic flutter'.

Why does it occur?

Treatment consists of complete rest: no attempt should be made to move the horse. Cooling should be attempted if at all possible; ideally fans to evaporate the sweat should achieve this. Cooling with ice-cold water has been said to risk causing the surface blood vessels to close down, thus preventing cooling of deeper tissues, but it is better than nothing. **Intravenous fluids** reverse any **dehydration** that would otherwise occur as the body loses fluid to the profuse sweating. In the case of diaphragmatic flutter, intravenous calcium, usually in the form of calcium borogluconate solution, corrects the deficiency.

How is it treated?

Ragwort poisoning 41

The reason why so many horses are poisoned by eating ragwort is that the plant is poisonous at all times of the year, and it is also poisonous even when dried in hay.

Why does it occur?

Ragwort poisoning is a cumulative poison, so eating a plant today and another plant next week produces the same effect as eating both on the same day. The plant has a bitter taste but horses will often eat it, especially in the spring when it is one of the earliest green plants to start growing, and in the heat of the summer when little grass is available. Once a horse does develop a taste for the plant it will eat it in preference to grass. This craving can return even after a prolonged period of stabling.

The alkaloids in ragwort are toxic to the horse's liver. The symptoms are of acute or chronic liver failure. Acutely the horse shows hepatic encephalopathy, the brain symptoms due to the high levels of ammonia in the blood as a result of the liver failure. The horse appears semi-conscious, standing pressing its head against the wall; it may be unable to stand. Chronic ragwort poisoning results in weight loss. Only in relatively mild cases is ragwort poisoning reversible in time. There is no antidote.

Is it treatable?

42 Kidney failure

What to look for

Compared with some other species, such as the cat or man, kidney failure is relatively rare in horses. When it does occur, the horse loses weight. It may drink more than normal, and pass more urine. A variety of different problems can cause the kidney damage: infection, causing abscesses; degeneration caused by bacterial toxins; damage caused by severe setfast; haemorrhage as a result of back injury.

How is it treated?

The kidney does not repair itself very well, and kidney disease is often progressive and fatal. No treatment is really possible, although anabolic **steroids** can provide some short-term help with the weight loss.

43 Narcolepsy

What to look for

Narcolepsy is the sudden onset of sleep in an active horse. The horse may become recumbent or it may just buckle at the knees, depending on the duration of the episode.

Why does it occur?

In some breeds narcolepsy runs in families. In other cases it is triggered off by an auto-immune reaction *ie* the horse becomes allergic to a part of its own body.

How is it treated?

Atropine gives short-term relief.

44 Epilepsy

What is it?

In the horse there are two forms of epilepsy: it can affect foals, in which case they often grow out of the problem; or it can affect adults, in which case it is usually due to the development of a lesion in the brain and is permanent.

Dilated pupil

What to look for

The epileptic seizures vary in their duration and their frequency. During a seizure the horse lies on its side, its legs moving involuntarily. The pupil is dilated. Although in some cases owners may come to recognise the warning signs, or to realise that particular stimuli may provoke a seizure, the horse may just collapse without warning. For this reason horses with epilepsy should not be ridden until treatment has kept them free from any seizures for six months.

How is it treated?

Treatment is aimed at preventing seizures rather than stopping a seizure that is already in progress, and may consist of the initial administration of diazapam, followed in the longer term by phenobarbitone.

Rabies

Rabies is not common in the horse, even in those parts of the world where the **virus** is widespread. Horses are not usually seen as a threat to human beings because even when affected they do not attack or bite other animals. As a result the international transport of horses does not usually require **vaccination** against rabies.

What is it?

Affected horses usually show the 'dumb' form of the disease. They appear depressed and stand with their head down. As the larynx becomes paralysed the neigh changes in character, and eventually the horse cannot even swallow to drink. The hind legs may become paralysed.

What to look for

There is no treatment for rabies, and affected horses are usually euthanased. Vaccination is used in countries where rabies is common, and is quite effective.

How is it treated?

Botulism

Botulism is caused not by eating food contaminated by the causal bacterium, *Clostridium botulinum*, but by eating food containing a toxin released from that organism. Like most clostridia, the organism likes to multiply away from oxygen, and botulism in horses has on a number of occasions been associated with big bale silage, where rodents have carried the bacterium deep into the acidic silage where conditions are ideal for it. Botulism can be contracted by drinking contaminated stagnant water.

What is it?

The toxin causes paralysis of the nerves, often starting with those of the larynx that are involved in swallowing. It spreads to the leg muscles, and ultimately to the muscles that are involved in breathing. There will be a loss of tone of the tail and the tongue, which hangs out of the mouth; because the horse has difficulty in swallowing, saliva drools from the mouth, and food/water, with food in the nostrils. The affected horse 'plays' in its feed and water buckets; it will develop a weak, shuffling gait, and muscle tremors appear as it tires.

What to look for

Penicillin can kill the bacterium, but it does not solve the problem of dealing with existing toxin. Antitoxin does exist, but is often not available in sufficiently large quantities to save the horse.

How is it treated?

47 Wobbler syndrome

What is it?

The name of the condition comes from the unsteadiness of the hindquarters that is often the first symptom. These symptoms are caused by pressure on the spinal cord in the horse's neck, but that pressure can arise from a number of different causes. In yearlings, wobbler syndrome can occur associated with a rich diet that results in uneven growth of the neck vertebrae. Older horses may also become wobblers: sometimes this is due to trauma to the vertebrae.

How is it treated?

A special restricted diet can in time allow growth abnormalities to even themselves out and some young horses recover, as long as they have not become paralysed. Radical surgery to remove the constricting bone can be attempted, with variable results. Horses mildly affected may still be able to race.

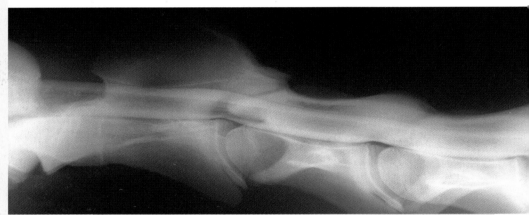

The spinal canal can be seen as a vertical tube, with a narrowing that produces pressure on the spinal cord

48 Protozoal encephalitis

What is it?

A number of areas in both North and South America have an almost epidemic incidence of encephalitis due to infection of the brain with protozoa. Horses may start symptoms suddenly, stumbling or falling without warning. They show generalised muscle weakness and become recumbent. As the disease progresses other nervous symptoms become evident, affecting the reflexes and skin sensitivity.

How is it treated?

Treatment with antiprotozoal drugs is possible but needs to be continued for very long periods if the horse is not to relapse, and this makes treatment very expensive. The disease is transmitted via the faeces, and it is thought that vermin then become an intermediate host. So vermin control and removal of faeces are important control measures.

Clostridium tetani is a bacterium that produces a deadly toxin. The problems start with spores gaining entry to a wound in either the skin or the bowel lining, such spores being common in soil. In low oxygen conditions, perhaps because of dying tissue, the spores change to the bacillus form of the organism and start multiplying. It is this form of the clostridium that produces the toxin, which in turn causes muscle spasms.

What is it?

These spasms can be triggered off by sudden noises, and may appear to involve all the muscles of the body. Holding the horse's head up characteristically causes a muscle spasm to pull the third eyelid across the eye. If the muscles involved in breathing become affected, then the condition becomes fatal. Although many other species of animal are affected with tetanus, horses are particularly susceptible to it.

What to look for

Penicillin kills the clostridium, but large doses of antitoxin are then needed to counter the toxin already produced. Intensive nursing, usually in quiet, dark surroundings to avoid stimuli, is needed to keep the horse alive whilst recuperation takes place. Because of their susceptibility, all horses should be vaccinated against tetanus; relying on the administration of antitoxins after the event is not a reliable alternative. Booster **vaccination**s are needed every 1–2 years after the primary course. The vaccine produces immunity against the toxin rather than the clostridium itself, and so is called a toxoid vaccine.

How is it treated?

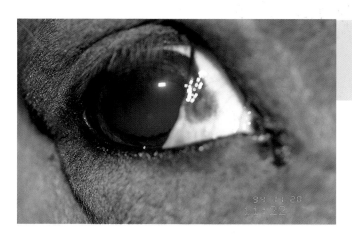

A horse with tetanus whose 'third eyelid' has opened out across almost half of the eyeball

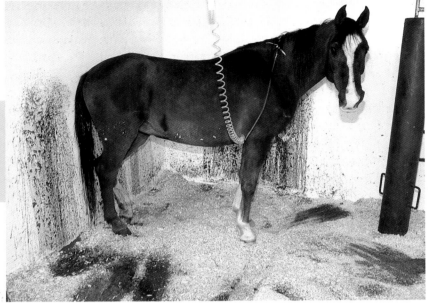

A horse receiving intravenous therapy to help combat dehydration as a result of acute salmonellosis. Note the walls stained by diarrhoea

What is it?

There are literally hundreds of different strains of salmonella **bacteria**, and they vary tremendously in their significance for the horse. Most cause no symptoms at all, but others can cause fever and profuse watery diarrhoea that leads to **dehydration** and often death. One problem is that horses can be symptomless carriers of the organism, which only multiplies so explosively when the horse is stressed eg after surgery, transport or antibiotic therapy. Salmonellosis is extremely infectious. The bacteria can survive for months or years in the stable environment, and once a stables has been involved in an outbreak it is extremely difficult to ever rid it of the organism. Because of the carrier state, where bacteria are present in some other part of the body besides the digestive tract, diagnosis is difficult. It may be necessary to culture faeces samples on numerous occasions before isolating a salmonella; and even then they do not grow well in the laboratory. Certainly one negative faecal culture is not sufficient to rule out the possibility of salmonella being present in the horse.

How is it treated?

Salmonellosis is a zoonosis ie it is a disease that can spread to human beings. It is also a disease that over the years has become resistant to many of the **antibiotics** currently available. In order to prevent further **drug resistance**, and in an attempt to ensure that there will always be effective drugs available for human beings, antibiotic therapy should only be a last resort. An antibiotic sensitivity test is essential before any antibiotic is used. Most fatalities are associated with dehydration, and intensive intravenous fluid therapy alone will usually keep the horse alive while the horse's own immune system deals with the bacteria.

No matter what its cause, profuse diarrhoea always poses a severe threat because the body cannot survive the resulting **dehydration**. Colitis X really refers to any acute inflammation of the bowel wall associated with diarrhoea that does not have a known cause. The symptoms are very similar to those of salmonellosis, and it may be that some cases are merely salmonellosis where faecal culture has been unsuccessful. Other cases are thought to reflect a sudden disturbance in the normal gut **bacterial** numbers and balance. Triggering factors such as high doses of **antibiotics** also point to this connection.

Without a precise cause, symptomatic treatment is obviously the only hope; intensive intravenous fluid therapy is needed to reverse the fluid and electrolyte loss in the diarrhoea. Hyosine **injections** slow bowel movements down, and codeine can also do this.

Granulomatous enteritis 52

Granulomatous enteritis has similarities to Crohn's disease in human beings. It occurs most commonly in young adult horses, sometimes in specific families, but the cause has not yet been determined.

The main symptom is weight loss. Although diarrhoea can occur, it is not common. The bowel wall becomes thickened and fails to absorb any nutrients, a deficiency that can be confirmed by a **glucose tolerance test**. Blood **albumen** levels are low. The prognosis in this condition is poor, and most cases become lethargic, lose their appetite and then die.

Steroids may temporarily reduce the inflammatory reaction in the gut wall, but they do not affect the ultimate outcome.

Intestinal worms 53

Horses suffer from both roundworms and tapeworms, although the former are the most numerous and the most troublesome.

There are three groups of roundworms: ascarids, large strongyles and small strongyles.

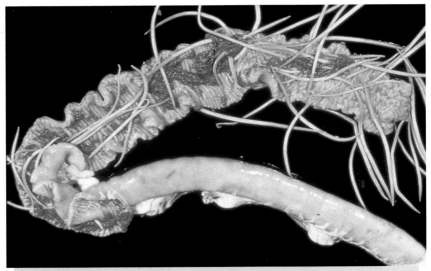

Large ascarid worms. Although a problem for foals, by adulthood most horses are immune

Roundworms

What are they?

There are three main groups of roundworm, the first of these being ascarids. The main ascarid worm in the horse is *Parascaris equorum*. It is principally a problem for foals, because with time the horse develops an immunity that prevents further worms developing. The foal picks up infective worm larvae from grazing. During their development the larvae migrate to the lungs and then up the trachea, or windpipe, to the larynx before being swallowed again and becoming adult worms in the intestines. These adults lay eggs which, by means of a thick protective coat, will survive on the pasture ready to hatch and infect next year's foals.

Large strongyles in faeces sample

The second group are the large strongyles, the principal of which being *Strongylus vulgaris*. It has a six-month-long life cycle. The larvae taken in during grazing migrate up the blood vessels that supply the intestines, until they reach the hub of the blood supply. Here they sit for several months, and during this time the blood supply to the intestine is often significantly decreased by the clot or embolism that forms where reaction around the larva decreases the diameter of the blood vessel. Digestive functions are correspondingly impaired. Eventually the larvae return to the intestines where they become adults. These cause further problems because they suck blood from the bowel wall, resulting in **anaemia**.

Large strongyles used to be a major cause of colic in the horse. In recent years, however, their significance has decreased drastically as modern wormers, such as the ivermectins, have been developed, that can even kill the migrating worm larvae.

There are many types of the third group, the small strongyle, or *cyathostome*. They may differ slightly anatomically, but their effect on the horse is basically the same. They have a short life cycle, lasting as little as 3–4 weeks, and so a horse will host several

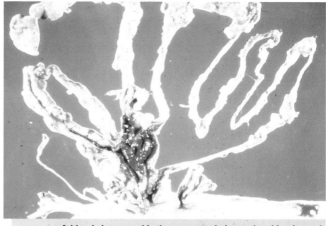

A blood clot caused by large strongyle larvae in a blood vessel

generations during each grazing season. The life cycle is simpler than in the large strongyle because the larvae do not migrate. After a short time in the gut wall as larvae, they emerge to become adult worms and complete the cycle.

Roundworms can cause weight loss because of damage to the intestines. They also cause respiratory problems such as coughing, a nasal discharge and a raised temperature, that are easily misdiagnosed as a respiratory viral infection. Regular worming every 6–8 weeks with most modern wormers will control the problem.

What to look for

Tapeworms

Tapeworms are more common in horses than was at first thought. *Anoplocephela* is the commonest tapeworm involved. It uses tiny mites on the herbage as its intermediate host, and the horse then takes these in as it grazes.

How do they occur?

The question is whether tapeworms cause any clinical problems or not. Recent research has shown that there is a connection between their presence, especially in the part of the bowel where the intestine and the caecum meet, and colic (especially impaction colic). The sensible advice is to dose horses against tapeworms using a double dose of pyrantel, every one or two years.

Symptoms to look for

Drugs resistance is an increasing problem with worms, but especially with the small strongyles.

How are they treated?

Tapeworm

Fenbendazole resistance is particularly widespread and products based on this drug (or other members of the benzamidazole family) should not be used unless checks are first carried out for the existence of resistance. Pyrantel only has limited resistance, and the ivermectin family little or no resistance. Changing your wormer every time you worm encourages the development of resistance, and it is better to stick to one effective drug for a year and then change to another. Worming too often may also speed up the development of resistance. You should time worming doses depending on both the grazing (stabled horses and horses at pasture during cold winter weather do not pick up any new worm larvae) and the wormer used (benzamidazole drugs will stop worm egg production for 3–6 weeks, but moxidectin will stop it for 13 weeks). Remember that the main effect of worming is to reduce the worm egg contamination of pasture, ie to reduce future problems.

Certain management techniques help to reduce worm problems: for instance, the regular removal of faeces from pastures; worming all horses on a farm at the same time; mechanically topping the grass, or grazing the grass with other animals to a uniform height, so that the horses then graze it evenly.

54 Cyathostomiasis

Why does it occur?

Recent years have seen an increasing incidence of a clinical condition known as cyathostomiasis. This occurs when large numbers of small strongyle larvae become dormant in the gut wall rather than continuing their life cycle. Factors that we don't understand cause enormous numbers of larvae to become active again in late autumn or spring, and they then emerge from the gut wall in large numbers within a very short time period. Naturally this causes severe damage to the bowel wall.

Cyathostomiasis can occur in late autumn or spring, and affected horses lose weight rapidly because the damaged bowel wall fails to absorb nutrients. Fluid balance is also upset and many of the horses develop watery diarrhoea. The condition can be fatal.

What to look for

Cyathostomiasis can occur even in horses that may have been wormed routinely. Wormers have most of their effect in the later part of the worm's life cycle, and so fail to prevent the dormancy occurring. Counting worm eggs in the faeces will fail to warn of the problem because the larvae

There may be only a few adult worms in the horse's droppings

aren't laying any eggs and although there may be large numbers of larvae there may only be low numbers of adult worms present. The presence of the larvae can be detected by carrying out specific protein electrophoresis on a blood sample to detect raised beta **globulin** levels. Intestinal alkaline phosphatase levels may also be increased due to the intestinal wall damage.

Treatment requires either a 5-day course of a high dose of fenbendazole, or a treatment with moxidectin (an ivermectin derivative). It may take some time for the horse to replace the weight loss because the intestinal wall cannot repair itself overnight.

How is it treated?

Liver disease 55

The liver is not only a very large organ, it is also very important for many different metabolic processes. It is involved in digestion and toxic waste removal. Repair of the damaged liver occurs only slowly, if at all. This means that significant liver damage is usually incurable. **Tumour**s, toxic chemicals, toxic plants and fatty infiltration are the commonest causes of chronic liver disease.

Why does it occur?

Chronic liver failure usually first shows by a progressive loss of weight. The horse loses its appetite. As the condition progresses horses often stand pressing their head against a wall, or stagger around aimlessly; this indicates that the central nervous system is affected, a condition known as hepatoencephalopathy: it is due to the build-up in the blood of toxic waste products that the liver would normally have dealt with. Confirmation of liver damage comes from finding raised blood levels of the enzymes aspartate aminotransferase (AST) and gamma glutamyl transpeptide (GGT). On the other hand, blood glucose levels may be low. A liver **biopsy** may provide evidence of the type of damage or its cause.

What to look for

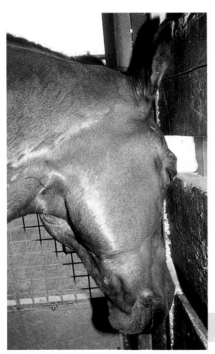

As mentioned earlier, there is little that can be done to reverse liver damage. A high **carbohydrate**, low protein diet with glucose and vitamin B supplements may help to compensate for the effects of liver failure.

How is it treated?

Head pressing into the corner of a stable, a classic symptom of hepatoencephalopathy

56 Navicular disease

Navicular disease is not actually a single disease with a single cause: it is a group of different scenarios that produce the same result, namely chronic lameness due to pain in the heel region of one or more feet.

How is it diagnosed?

The first step to a diagnosis of navicular disease is proving that the pain causing the lameness is in the posterior half of the foot. Using a nerve block that removes sensation from only that part of the foot does this. Confirmation of the diagnosis then most commonly comes from x-rays. In many cases there is definite pathology visible in the navicular bone; in others, vets have to resort to grading the amount of x-ray change, with inevitably a number of borderline cases. Increasingly the solution is to inject local anaesthetic directly into the navicular bursa, using x-rays to ensure that the needle is in the right place. This confirms the diagnosis even in those cases where there are no bony changes visible on x-ray.

Navicular disease is essentially a degenerative joint disease like any other, but complicated by both the pressure on the back of the navicular bone from the deep flexor tendon and by specific blood supply problems to the bone. It often first shows itself clinically after either a period of rest – for instance, whilst lame from another cause – or following a change of ownership or of farrier, or after a change to a different riding activity. Poor foot balance and shoeing are major contributory causes.

One of the complications is that the x-ray changes that we associate with the disease can also be found in sound horses. Thus when looking at x-rays from an otherwise sound horse whose purchase is being contemplated, it can be difficult to say 'this horse has navicular disease'. We also know that if horses diagnosed as having navicular disease subsequently go sound as a result of treatment, the x-ray changes will remain even after the return to soundness.

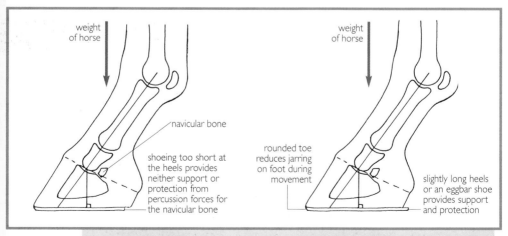

weight of horse

navicular bone

shoeing too short at the heels provides neither support or protection from percussion forces for the navicular bone

weight of horse

rounded toe reduces jarring on foot during movement

slightly long heels or an eggbar shoe provides support and protection

The effects of good and bad shoeing on the navicular area

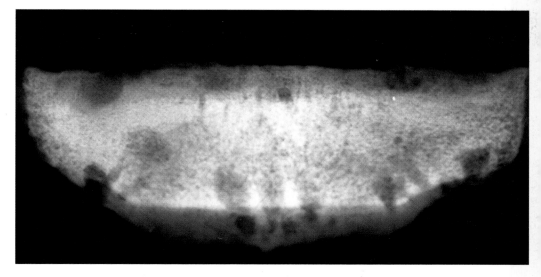

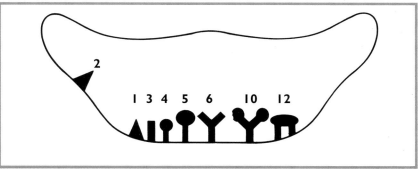

The x-ray (*top*) shows the damage to the navicular bone. The dark shadows around the lower edge of the navicular bone represent alterations in blood supply to the bone. The diagram is an attempt to score the severity of the disease

How is it treated?

The basic treatment for the condition consists of correct foot balancing, especially correction of a long toe/short heel conformation, and remedial shoeing. The aim is to take weight away from the heel region of the foot where the navicular bone is situated, and to this end, eggbar shoes are commonly used. Isoxuprine may be given to increase the blood supply to the area, but its use is no substitute for correct foot balance. Surgery to cut the collateral ligaments supporting the navicular bone so that it can achieve a slightly different and less painful position, may be helpful in some cases. Injecting **steroids** and local anaesthetics directly into the navicular bursa may also return the horse to soundness. Phenylbutazone is the painkiller/**anti-inflammatory** drug most commonly used, and its permanent use may be the only way of keeping an affected horse sound.

Over the years there has been controversy as to whether navicular disease is hereditary or not. Current thinking is that a condition with so many contributing factors cannot be hereditary in itself; nevertheless, the foot conformation, gait and so on, that lead to the development of the disease, may have hereditary aspects.

57 Sore shins

Why does it occur?

A horse's shin is the front of the cannon bone. Young horses that are put into fast work before their bones are structurally mature may develop pain in the region. The condition is commonest in young racehorses, where the immature bone reacts to the percussion forces during galloping by an inflammatory reaction.

What to look for

The area may feel warm, and a further consequence is the production of more immature bone over the shin in an attempt to support the stressed area. In severe cases stress fractures of this surface bone can occur.

Affected horses are lame, although because two or more legs are usually involved this might not be obvious to an inexperienced observer. The gait will be stiff.

How is it treated?

Rest is essential for such horses. Cold applications and **anti-inflammatory drugs** will help to reduce the inflammation, but they should not be used simply to mask the problem so that the horse can continue in work. Laser therapy or pulsed electromagnetic field therapy have also been useful. Even when the horse returns to soundness it should not be worked at speed or on hard ground for some weeks if a recurrence is to be avoided.

58 OCD

What is it?

Osteochondritis dessicans, or OCD, is a joint problem that usually becomes evident when a horse first goes into hard work, so it is a problem of two- to three-year-old racehorses or four- to five-year-old competition horses. However, OCD has its origins during the first six months of a foal's life, when the bones are growing rapidly and the articular cartilage of the joints is maturing. A localised deficit in the blood supply to the

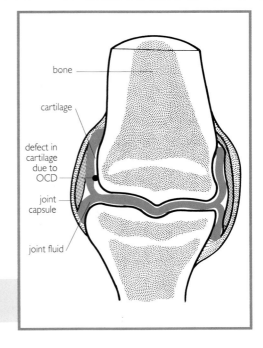

bone

cartilage

defect in cartilage due to OCD

joint capsule

joint fluid

The point of weakness in the joint

bone leads to a weak area of cartilage. At a later date the stress of work causes either a flap of cartilage to become mobile, or a fragment of bone and cartilage to break away into the joint cavity. It is at this stage that the horse becomes lame. The joint capsule may be swollen by an increased amount of joint fluid, but it is not warm or otherwise inflamed. Unlike many causes of lameness, OCD can cause sudden lameness in a horse that is just resting in its stable.

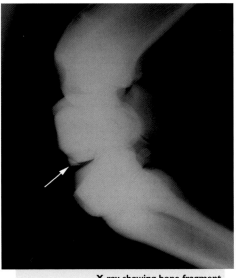

X-ray showing bone fragment

When a bone fragment does break off, this will be visible on x-ray. Otherwise diagnosis relies on using an arthroscope to actually see the cartilage defects. Treatment then consists of scraping away all the defective cartilage. Interestingly, although this leaves raw bone exposed, it is not painful and the horse has a good chance of becoming sound again. Many specific lameness problems, such as spavin, start as OCD, and eventually lead to degenerative joint disease years later.

How is it treated?

Chip fractures 59

Moving joints are subjected to great pressures, and sometimes bone at the edge of the articular surfaces breaks off. Such chip fractures may still be partially attached by cartilage or they may float free in the joint fluid.

Why does it occur?

Not all chip fractures cause pain and lameness. It is therefore sometimes wise to carry out intra synovial **anaesthesia** to prove that a specific joint is actually responsible for any lameness. If this is the case, then removal of the chip is necessary. This is often carried out using a special endoscope called an arthroscope. It may be possible to screw very large chips back into place.

How is it treated?

Pyramidal disease is a specific chip fracture where the extensor tendon that attaches to the front of the pedal bone just by the coffin joint pulls the pyramidal process off the pedal bone. Screw fixation of the piece of bone is needed so that the tendon can work properly again.

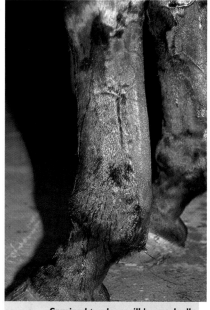

Sprained tendons will be markedly increased in diameter

What are they?

Tendons are fibrous structures that are attached at one end to a muscle and at the other end to a bone: their function is to transfer the pull from the muscle in order to move the bone. As the horse does not have any muscles lower down the leg than the knee or the hock, the major tendons associated with walking, trotting, galloping and so on, are relatively long. They are also relatively susceptible to injury. Ligaments have basically the same microscopic structure as tendons, but their job is to join two bones together.

What to look for

When tendons are damaged there are classic symptoms of inflammation: the area is hot, painful and swollen, with inflammatory fluid separating the previously tightly packed tendon fibres, increasing the cross-sectional area of the tendon but also drastically weakening it mechanically. Individual fibres – which are made up of a protein called collagen – are damaged and torn. The most common site of tendon damage is down the back of the cannon bone, especially of the front legs, but any tendon or ligament is susceptible. The superficial and deep flexor tendons down the cannon usually become sprained during fast work, when landing after a jump, or following a sudden uncontrolled movement on uneven ground. They are almost at the limit of their normal elasticity during fast work, so it takes relatively little to push them past that limit.

How is it treated?

The first treatment for a recent tendon injury is cold therapy, to reduce the blood flow to the affected area, and so in turn reduce the amount of inflammatory fluid formed. The horse should have stable rest in order to prevent further damage. **Anti-inflammatory** agents will help, and will reduce the pain. There is some evidence that polysulphated glycosaminoglycan is also helpful in these early couple of weeks. The horse starts with just five minutes in-hand walking exercise twice daily. Recovery from a sprained tendon is slow, and it will be six to nine months before the horse is back in work again. The exercise will increase gradually during this time, the aim being to provide some tension to the new tendon fibres that are forming in an attempt to encourage them to be laid down in the direction of natural tension rather than in the irregular pattern that would otherwise form.

Ultrasound scans have a vital role to play in showing us, the extent of tendon damage, and then the progress in repairing that damage. Damaged areas where there is inflammatory fluid and blood clot show as black areas on the scan. It is possible to measure the degree of enlargement of the tendon's cross-sectional area using ultrasound, and to see when regular parallel alignment of tendon fibres has replaced the initial irregular repair.

A great number of therapies have been used to try and speed up tendon repair. There is now an understanding that nothing will achieve this, but that we can improve the quality of repair and so decrease the chance of further injury. **Laser therapy** helps to reduce the swelling of the tendon sheath and other tissues around the tendon, and it has been claimed that **magnetic field therapy** helps ensure better alignment of the new fibres. Hydrotherapy is used during convalescence to help the muscles involved become fit again without putting strain on the tendon.

Surgical splitting of the damaged tendon during the early stages still has its supporters, who claim that it allows the inflammatory fluid to escape, rather than being forced between the fibres. There is a constant search for drugs that will improve healing. Bapten helps to stop the initial irregular replacement fibres becoming consolidated, but it does not seem to be the panacea for tendon repair that it was initially thought to be.

It is difficult to tell when a sprained tendon has recovered enough to withstand fast work. If the tendon is not ready to withstand the controlled exercise of work, then it is not ready to withstand the uncontrolled strains of being turned out in a field. Ultrasound evidence of healing is the best indication we have, but eventually we have to take a chance and work normally again. There is a danger period about nine months after the injury when the tendon on the corresponding healthy leg will come under strain, and be prone to injury. The slightest sign of heat or thickening of this tendon should be taken seriously, reducing exercise and using cold therapy until it settles.

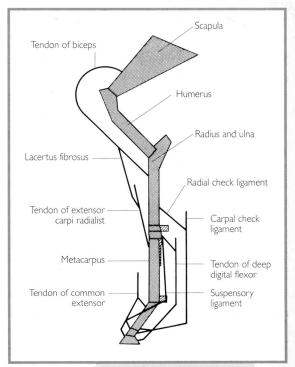

The tendons of the front leg

Tendon of biceps
Scapula
Humerus
Radius and ulna
Lacertus fibrosus
Radial check ligament
Tendon of extensor carpi radialist
Carpal check ligament
Metacarpus
Tendon of deep digital flexor
Tendon of common extensor
Suspensory ligament

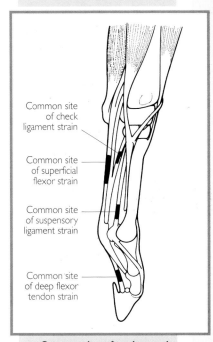

Common sites of tendon sprain

Common site of check ligament strain
Common site of superficial flexor strain
Common site of suspensory ligament strain
Common site of deep flexor tendon strain

Atrial fibrillation

This is a heart rhythm irregularity that causes a lack of exercise tolerance. The loss of control of the contractions of the atrial chamber in the heart results in a fast, irregular heartbeat. The resulting circulation of blood may be sufficient for the horse to function perfectly normally at rest, but when stressed it may have difficulty in breathing. A **pulse** may be visible up the large jugular vein in the neck. Sometimes oedema occurs in the legs.

How is it treated? Quinidine sulphate slows the electrical impulses from the atrium to the heart's ventricle, which actually pumps the blood. Normal rhythm may be achieved as a result but the drug carries a risk of side effects that cause breathing difficulties, so great care has to be taken in establishing the correct dose. Treatment may need to be permanent.

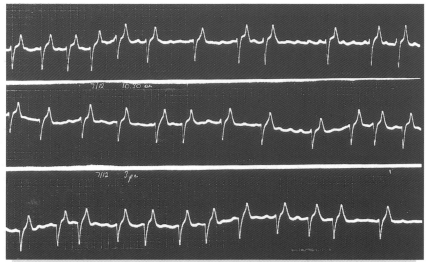

The fast contractions of the atrium seen on this electrocardiogram are not separated by signs of ventricular contraction

Everyone knows that arteries take the blood to the tissues, and the veins carry it back to the heart. Fewer people understand that there is also another system draining tissue fluid back to the general circulation, comprising very thin-walled vessels called lymphatics. If the lymphatic drainage is blocked, tissue fluid accumulates and the area becomes swollen with oedema.

Lymphangitis is an inflammatory process that either blocks the lymphatics (perhaps by a swollen lymph gland) or makes the lymphatic wall permeable so that the fluid leaks out. It is usually the drainage from the hind legs that is involved. Sometimes the condition has been called Monday Morning Disease because horses were found with such swollen hind legs after the Sunday rest day, but the same name is also confusingly applied to azoturia. Affected horses may be stiff, lethargic and running a temperature.

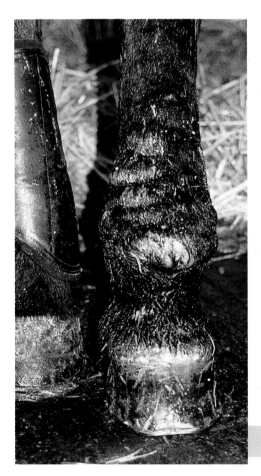

Skin stretched by oedema oozes lymph, or tissue fluid

Treatment consists of **diuretics** to encourage a reduction in tissue fluid, **anti-inflammatory drugs**, and hot **fomentations** may help the drainage by encouraging the general circulation. Sometimes the **lymph glands** in the groin or the inguinal region are swollen, when they should be fomented. Gentle walking exercise will help the leg circulation.

Once a horse has suffered from lymphangitis it is more prone to further attacks because the cells that form the wall of the lymphatics may not ever heal completely.

63 Purpura haemorrhagica

What is it?

Purpura is caused by an immune reaction following a **bacterial** disease, most commonly strangles. The reaction damages the blood vessel walls. This in turn causes oedema of the legs, and the appearance of small **haemorrhages** on the pink mucous membranes of the eyes, tongue, lips and gums. The horse is very lethargic and may have a slight temperature. Oedema of the lung causes coughing and difficulty in breathing. Purpura can be fatal.

How is it treated?

Treatment consists of large doses of **antibiotics** to make sure that any remaining bacteria are killed. At the same time a prolonged course of **steroids** will reduce the immune reaction. Gentle exercise will help the general circulation.

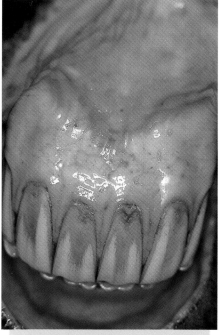

The pin head sized haemorrhages are easy to see on this horse's upper gum

64 Kissing spines

What is it?

Back problems are not as common as some horse owners and back manipulators would have us believe. The condition known as 'kissing spines' is probably the most common long-lasting back problem. The spines in question are the dorsal spines of the horse's vertebrae, and the 'kissing' refers to the contact between adjacent spines when new bone forms. Vertebrae all along the back can be involved, although the area just behind the saddle is perhaps most commonly affected.

What to look for

The back pain can show itself in many ways. It might be through poor performance, or there might be obvious pain when a part of the back is pressed or when the horse is ridden. The bony changes are visible on x-ray, but a powerful machine is necessary for good images. The bony reaction can settle down completely with a full recovery of performance, so finding changes on x-ray does not necessarily mean that the horse still has a problem. Nuclear scintigraphy will show if there is active bone activity or not. Other parts of the back may be painful as well, because muscle spasm occurs as the horse braces its back against the pain.

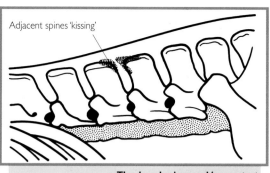

Adjacent spines 'kissing'

The dorsal spines making contact

Six months' rest is the best treatment of choice for kissing spines. If the bony reaction is still active after that time, then surgery is possible to remove the top portion of one of the spines involved; this will prevent pressure on the tip of the adjacent process.

How is it treated?

Fractured pelvis 65

The pelvis is actually a number of bones fused together, and the effect of a fracture depends on which part of the pelvis is broken. The wing of the illium projects on each side of the body and can be easily felt and seen. A fracture here may leave the horse still able to stand and walk. Some horses even develop a fibrous healing of the fracture site in time. Unfortunately fractures of the central part of the pelvis often also involve damage to other vital structures as well. In this case the horse may be unable to stand.

Why does it occur?

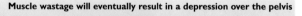

Muscle wastage will eventually result in a depression over the pelvis

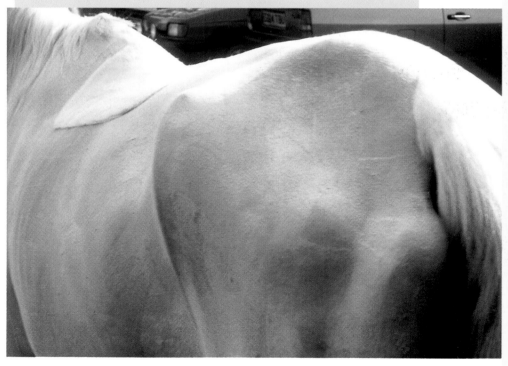

66 Barker foals

What is it? There are a number of names for the problem that occurs when foals are born with incomplete maturation of their respiratory and other systems. The scientific name is neonatal maladjustment syndrome. A lack of the chemicals that cover the lung surfaces means that oxygen absorption is poor. Some of these foals make a harsh noise that resulted in the name 'barker'. Other cases can appear completely unaware of their surroundings. They will have convulsions and are weak. We now know that some of these foals can survive and lead a normal life. However, this will usually require intensive nursing, including oxygen therapy, to keep them alive until their body systems have matured to an appropriate level of functionality.

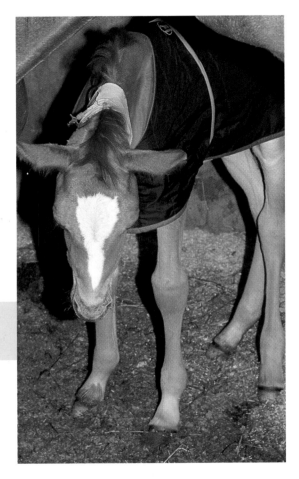

This is classic symptoms of a Barker foal: head down, depressed, uninterested and unaware of his surroundings

67 Sleepy foal disease

What is it? This rather old-fashioned term was used to indicate any disease that made the foal lethargic without any other symptoms. As such it came to mean any as yet undiagnosed infectious disease that was causing a raised temperature but few other symptoms. Sometimes the causal agent is never diagnosed, the foal recovering in response to **antibiotics** that kill the **bacteria**.

The joints of young foals are particularly susceptible to localised infections. In many cases the **bacteria** gain entry through the umbilical cord during the first day or two of life, circulate in the bloodstream and finally end up in a small blood vessel in a joint. From here they enter the joint capsule and multiply rapidly because they no longer have contact with the protective antibodies from the bloodstream. The joint becomes hot and swollen with **pus**. Bacteria then start to enter the bloodstream in large numbers; the foal develops a high temperature, and stops suckling.

What is it?

Draining the pus from the joint and flushing out the remaining toxins with saline increases the chances of recovery of normal joint function. High doses of **antibiotics** are necessary to kill the infection: the swelling around the joint reduces the normal penetration of drugs into the joint. In some cases the destructive substances in the pus damage the joint cartilage beyond recovery, leaving the foal permanently lame if a leg joint has been involved.

How is it treated?

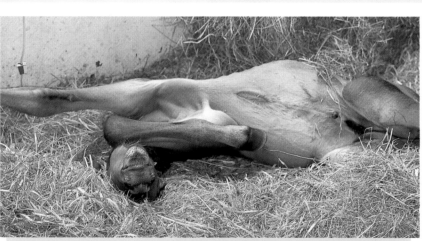

A foal will eventually experience severe pain from retained meconium

During the months that the foal spends growing inside its dam it produces both faeces and urine. The small amount of faeces that accumulates inside its colon is called meconium, and it must be passed within a day or two of the foal's birth. It is sticky in texture, and orange or black in colour, and there is usually about 45cm (18in) in length to pass.

What is it?

    The first sign that a foal has retained meconium is usually that it stands with its tail held up but does not pass faeces or urine. It then stops suckling and develops

115

a temperature, and quickly becomes lethargic. Colt foals suffer the condition more frequently than fillies.

Reasonably urgent treatment is required because the absorption of toxins can be fatal. The meconium has to be expelled completely. Mini enemas inserted into the foal's rectum will usually soften the meconium and stimulate its expulsion. In extreme cases surgical removal may be necessary. Nursing is important to keep the foal hydrated during the illness despite the absence of suckling.

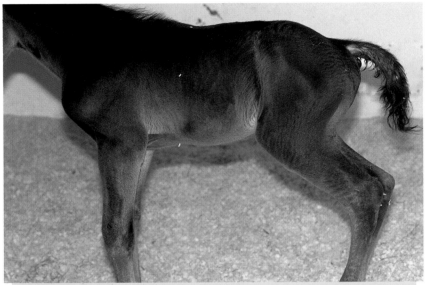

Note the raised tail as this foal tries unsuccessfully to pass meconium

70 Ruptured bladder

Rupture of the bladder usually becomes evident within the first two to three days of life, although the trauma that causes the rupture is usually the delivery itself. Colts are more susceptible than fillies. As the foal's abdomen fills with urine, the foal has colic and stops suckling. The abdomen becomes swollen with the accumulation of urine.

Treatment ultimately consists of the surgical repair of the rupture, and it may be necessary to drain the urine from the abdomen to help the foal become fit for **anaesthesia**. It may be some time after surgery before one can be sure that the urine did not cause serious damage to the other organs in the abdomen.

Sometimes a foal that is born perfectly healthy becomes ill within a few days. It becomes **jaundiced** and may have blood in its urine.

What to look for

The **anaemia** is due to the destruction of the foal's red blood cells by antibodies that formed in the mare's circulation against foal red blood cells that have leaked into her bloodstream during pregnancy. When the foal suckles the colostrum during the first 24–48 hours of life it can absorb these and other antibodies, leading in this case to the destruction of large numbers of its red blood cells.

What is it?

The first part of treatment is to prevent the foal having any more access to its mother's milk. A blood transfusion may be necessary in severe cases to replace the red blood cells lost. Obviously the donor should not be a close relative of the foal, and no more than one transfusion should be given without full blood typing to ensure compatibility of the donor blood.

How is it treated?

A mare may be predisposed to the development of foal blood antibodies by the large amount of leakage that occurs from her placenta. A blood test during late pregnancy can detect the antibodies in advance: it is then sufficient to prevent the foal suckling for the first few days until its intestines are no longer able to absorb the potentially dangerous antibodies. Because a lack of colostrum also means that the foal will be susceptible to infections, gamma **globulin** preparations or colostrum from another mare should be given.

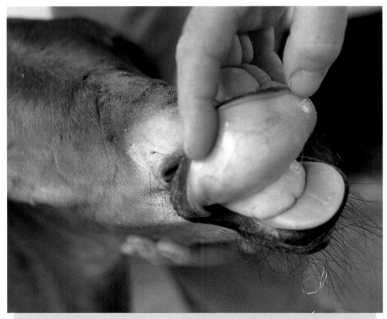

The membranes of this foal are yellow and jaundiced, a clear sign of anaemia

72 Lungworm

The lungworm, *Dictyocaulus arnfieldi*, is interesting because it hardly ever causes any symptoms in donkeys but can cause serious problems in horses. Affected horses therefore usually have a history of contact with donkeys or their grazing.

In horses the parasite causes coughing and a nasal discharge. Because the reaction in the airways to the worms is so great they constrict, causing symptoms similar to COPD. Fortunately the incidence of clinical cases has decreased greatly in recent years because of the widespread use of ivermectin wormers, which are effective against the parasite.

Donkeys may pass lungworm to horses that share their grazing

73 Pleurisy

The condition relates to an infection of the membranes lining the chest and covering the outer surface of the lungs. **Pus** accumulates in the space between the lungs and the chest wall. The horse's breathing becomes fast and shallow, and its temperature is high. The infection may multiply so rapidly that the horse dies.

Treatment requires drainage of the pus. High doses of antibiotic are necessary to eradicate the infection.

Although this viral disease is centred on Africa, global warming may lead to a spread of the mosquitoes and biting midges that carry the infection to other parts of the world. There are nine strains of the **virus** (see **bacteria/virus**) and immunity to one strain does not protect against infection with another, which is one reason why it spreads so rapidly in horse populations.

Infected horses have a fever. This may be followed by sudden death. Because the disease affects the walls of blood vessels and allows fluid to leak out into the surrounding tissues, some horses develop a cough due to fluid in the lungs. Others develop subcutaneous oedema and a **heart murmur**.

There is no treatment for the condition; however, there are very strict international measures to prevent its spread. Vaccines are available, but they do not provide protection between strains of the virus.

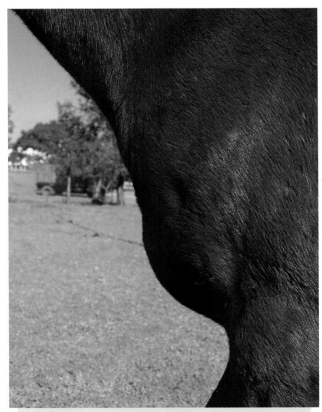

Swollen areas of oedema in the brisket

Sweet itch

Ridges of thick skin along the neck and withers of a horse suffering from sweet itch

What is it?

Sweet itch is an allergic disease. The horse becomes hypersensitive to the saliva injected into the skin by the *Culicoides* biting midges. The intense irritation makes the horse rub the areas bitten by the midge, usually the mane and tail. The hair is rubbed off and the skin rubbed so raw that it oozes **serum** (see **plasma/serum**). This disease occurs in the summer when the midges are active, but it will take months for the hair to regrow during autumn and winter.

How is it treated?

Although benzyl benzoate applied to the affected areas is soothing and may be a deterrent, treatment really depends on preventing the midges biting the horse. Besides the use of insect repellents, this involves stabling the horse during those times that the midges are most active (the first and last few hours of daylight). In severe cases the horse has to be stabled with a mosquito netting protecting the stable. Once the symptoms occur, only **steroids** appear able to completely remove the irritation, and their use has to be undertaken with caution because they may trigger off laminitis, especially in ponies. Once a horse has sweet itch it will continue to suffer from it in succeeding years, usually getting worse every year.

76 Lice

What are they?

There are two types of lice, biting lice and sucking lice, but the symptoms are basically the same, namely irritation that causes the horse to rub itself. Patches of hair will be rubbed away and the skin may be rubbed raw. The neck and shoulder areas are probably the worst affected.

Lice breed in the long winter coat and feed on skin debris and body fluids. The itching they cause will make the horse or pony rub the most affected areas, usually the neck and shoulders, also the tail. The resulting bald or matted areas are seen in the mid to late winter

Lice do not live long off the horse. During the summer they are least active, and the symptoms tend to disappear; they are most active during cold weather in horses with a thick coat. Spread from horse to horse usually requires direct contact.

Anti-parasitic dusting powders and **shampoos** are available, but they need weekly or monthly application because they rarely remove 100 per cent of the lice. Ivermectin wormers kill lice during the first twenty-four hours after their use. Clipping the coat removes the shelter used by the lice.

How is it treated?

Ringworm

What is it?

Ringworm is a non-itching fungal skin disease. Because the **fungi** (usually members of the Trichophyton or Microsporum families) affect the skin and the base of the hairs, hairs break off at skin level, leaving bald areas. Typically these areas appear circular in shape, but ringworm does not always have such a convenient form. There may be small irregular areas anywhere on the body, or just occasional hairs might be affected.

Ringworm can survive for months or years in the environment because it forms spores that are resistant to extremes of temperature. Thus a horse may be infected for weeks or months before any symptoms appear. In fact horses will eventually cure themselves by developing an immunity to the fungus, and it is this fact that has led to the popularity of a number of folk remedies for the disease, which appear to work because some time after their use the symptoms disappear. These remedies include the application of sump oil and other noxious substances.

The antibiotic griseofulvin given orally may kill the fungus but it has side effects. Anti-fungal washes are available. Strict hygiene must be employed for grooming kit, tack, horseboxes, stables and so on, to prevent the fungus spreading by contact.

Not all ringworm lesions are circular areas of hair loss

How is it treated?

78 Habronemiasis

What is it?

Parasitic worms don't only cause internal problems. Habronema worms that live in the stomach are acquired by the horse when the biting fly that acts as their intermediate host lands on moist areas of the horse's skin – around open wounds, the eyes or the tip of the penis. The larvae leave the fly's mouthparts and establish themselves in the skin, where they stimulate inflammation. Clinically we see raised, ulcerated areas that do not heal.

How is it treated?

Ivermectin wormers kill off the larvae and the adult worms in the stomach. **Steroids** may be necessary to reduce the inflammatory reaction, and very large areas may even need to be removed surgically.

79 Parasitic microfilaria

What is it?

Unlike most parasitic worms, *Onchocerca cervicalis* does not live in the digestive tract but in the large ligament, the *ligamentum nuchae*, in the neck. The worm produces microscopic microfilaria that migrate to the skin and eyelids. The parasites' lifecycle is completed by midges picking up the microfilaria from one horse and transmitting them to another horse that they bite.

What to look for

Some, but by no means all, horses become hypersensitive to the microfilaria in the skin. The first symptom is loss of hair, and then a scaly patch that causes the horse irritation. Microfilaria may inhibit the healing of skin wounds from other causes, and when they are present in the eyelids they can cause a discharge from the eye due to the irritation.

How is it treated?

The parasites are killed by ivermectin, although it may take a couple of months for the lesions to resolve. Care will need to be taken when eye lesions are present to avoid side effects.

A typical non-healing wound associated with microfiliaria

The first thing to say about mud fever is that this skin infection occurs not only in wet muddy conditions that lead to the superficial skin layers becoming sodden and traumatised, but also in dry, dusty conditions where there is a sandpaper-like effect that in similar fashion produces areas of broken skin. The infection is caused by two organisms: the first is called *Dermatophilus congolensis* and is almost halfway between a bacterium and a fungus; the second, and possibly the most important, is the staphylococcus **bacteria**.

The infection destroys the surface skin layers, leaving a raw, oozing surface. The exudate dries to form a scab, which then protects the underlying oozing area from both the environment and from our attempts to treat the mud fever. As a general rule, if the scabs are very painful and tightly stuck to the horse's skin, then it is probably a staphylococcus infection. The lower legs are the area usually affected, although in severe cases the infection can extend up to the underparts of the body. As the infection extends deeper through the skin layers it can cause cellulitis, with swelling extending up the leg. Less observant horse owners might mistake mud fever lesions on the back of the pastern for an overreach wound.

The first stage of treatment is to remove all the scabs that have formed, and this is easier said than done. The horse may need sedating to allow you to do it, but every single one needs to be removed. Soaking the scabs with lukewarm antiseptic

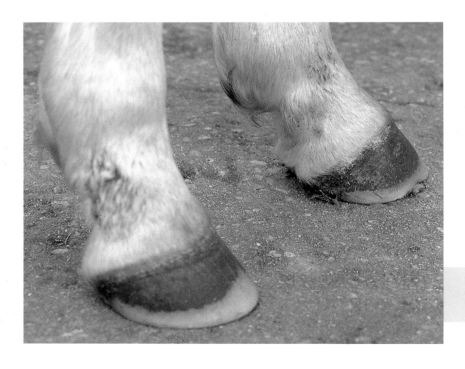

Mud fever lesions on the back of the pasterns

solution such as chlorhexidine may help; or try rubbing on a liberal coating of baby oil (for human babies!) — this softens the scabs which, after a couple of hours or the morning after, can generally be easily rubbed off with the fingers. The hairs need clipping away so that they cannot provide anchorage for future scabs. The affected area should then be kept scrupulously dry and free of scabs. In many cases that is sufficient, because Dermatophilus cannot survive drying whilst it is active, although it can produce spores that can resist drying. Often we apply antibiotic preparations to the affected area and surrounding skin. Dermatophilus is sensitive to most **antibiotics**, but it is no use applying them to scabbed areas where they will not come into contact with the active organisms.

Some owners use petroleum jelly or oily ointments to provide a waterproof layer over the skin. The problem with this approach is that it protects the organisms from drying and so encourages their multiplication. Such ointments should only be used *after* the Dermatophilus has been killed and new scabs are no longer being formed, as a preventive measure against further infection.

Staphylococcus infections can be more difficult to treat because the bacteria invade the hair follicles deep in the skin surface. Drugs such as potassium iodide can help to flush out the follicles and soften the scabs.

81 Rain scald

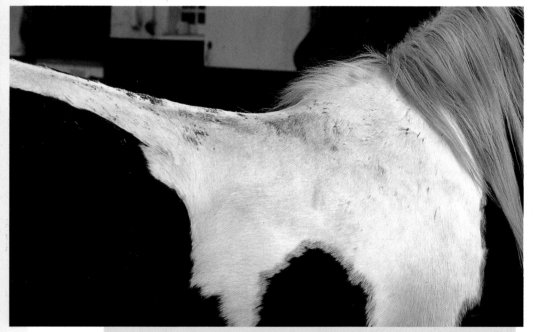

Rain scald will produce lesions, especially over the withers and shoulder area

Dermatophilus causes two superficial skin infections in the horse: rain scald and mud fever. Rain scald takes its name from the fact that it often appears after a horse has been out in the rain, especially during mild temperatures. The wet conditions wash the Dermatophilus spores over the upper parts of the horse's body and wherever they find a microscopic break in the skin they become active and multiply. The result is numerous small scabs on the skin that hold the hairs together in tufts, like small paintbrushes. Sometimes the affected areas exactly follow the pattern of the rain as it runs off the neck, shoulders and body.

What is it?

Antiseptic shampoos will usually kill the infection, though take care to dry the horse thoroughly afterwards. A 5 per cent copper sulphate solution used as a wash is probably a cheaper alternative.

How is it treated?

Poisonous plants 82

Yew twigs and leaves are especially poisonous to horses. It is not unknown for horses to be found with half-chewed leaves stll in their mouths

There are a number of plants that are common in a particular geographical area, but are nevertheless poisonous to herbivores such as the horse. It is only possible to deal with some of these in a book such as this.

What are they?

Acorns are poisonous, as are oak leaves, due to their tannin content. They cause constipation and a gastro-enteritis that ultimately may lead to severe diarrhoea. Tannin also causes kidney damage.
Treatment: This consists of liquid paraffin via a **stomach tube** to speed up the removal of the large number of acorns that have often been consumed. Beware that

Acorns

acorns from a tree in a neighbouring field can still be blown into your paddock.

Yew

Yew tree poisoning is perhaps the quickest poison: animals may be found dead with the leaves still in their mouth. Rather unusually the bright red berries are not poisonous, only the twigs and leaves.
Treatment: There is none.

St John's Wort

There are a number of plants, such as St John's Wort, that cause a particular type of liver damage which results in the horse becoming hypersensitive to sunlight. The photosensitisation results in blisters forming on the white, unpigmented areas of skin; the muzzle is particularly susceptible. Owners may not notice lesions on white skin around the coronet if the grass is tall.
Treatment: The horse should be stabled to protect it from the sun and to prevent access to the plants. When it does go outside again, sun-block cream should be applied to any white areas.

Selenium poisoning

Some plants have a specific ability to accumulate selenium from the soil, especially in areas where the soil levels are unusually high anyway. The plant will be dangerous even when dried in hay. Acutely, selenium poisoning causes nervous symptoms and death, but plants more commonly cause a chronic condition known as chronic alkali disease. Hair is lost from the mane and tail, and laminitis occurs because of a serious decrease in hoof horn quality.

Bracken and horsetail are poisonous to horses. They are not usually eaten if there is other herbage available, but unusually they are more palatable when dried in hay. In these plants the toxic principle destroys vitamin B thiamine in the body and causes a deficiency. Clinically the horse becomes ataxic and stops eating. It may develop convulsions and then die.
Treatment: Large doses of thiamine usually result in a rapid recovery.

83 Rotavirus

What is it?

There is some discussion over whether members of the rotavirus family actually do cause clinical disease in their own right. They are certainly isolated from foals with diarrhoea, but they can also be found in apparently healthy foals. It probably ultimately depends on the numbers present as to whether they have an effect or not. The virus is taken in through the mouth; it is very resistant, and can survive for long periods in stables and pasture.

What to look for

Diarrhoea, associated with a loss of suck, and sometimes colic. Many cases do not recover spontaneously, but **vaccination** is possible.

The pedal bone is well protected inside the hoof, but severe trauma can still cause its fracture. The horse becomes suddenly lame, and may be unwilling to take any weight on the leg. **Nerve blocks** pinpoint the foot as the cause of the lameness, and the fracture is diagnosed by **radiography**.

What is it?

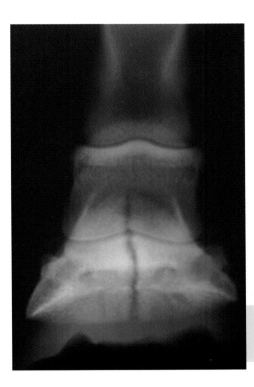

In some cases box rest will allow the fracture to heal, using the hoof as a splint. Other cases require surgery to screw the two or more fragments of bone together. The screw is inserted via a window cut through the hoof wall. The screw may require removal after the fracture has healed because reaction may occur around the screw head.

How is it treated?

An x-ray showing a vertical fracture down the middle of the pedal bone

When a horse stands on a nail or a sharp flint it may puncture the sole. A wrongly placed horseshoe nail can do the same.

How does it occur?

The horse is lame for a short period but then becomes sound again, in the same way as a needle prick only hurts us temporarily. In the majority of horses though the puncture wound is also infected and **bacteria** start to multiply inside or underneath the sole. A day or two later the horse suddenly goes acutely lame because the **pus** that has formed is pressing on the sensitive laminae inside the foot. The horse will often refuse to take any weight on the leg, giving rise to concerns that there may even be a fracture present. The hoof may be warm to the touch.

What to look for

A close examination of the surface of the sole after it has been cleaned thoroughly, and perhaps the surface horn pared away, will hopefully reveal a black mark. This is the puncture site. It is black because the pus that forms in the hoof, away from contact with the air, is usually black or grey. Pressure on the area will not only be painful but may squeeze out a small amount of pus.

How is it treated?

Treatment starts with cutting away the horn around the puncture site until good drainage is achieved. Sometimes the pus is powdery rather than liquid, and if so it should all be cut away. The hoof should be poulticed until 24–48 hours after any pus drains out. If there is any fear

A large area of sole has been under-run

that the infection is spreading eg if there is any swelling of the pastern, antibiotic cover is needed. When the horse is sound again the hole should be plugged either with Stockholm Tar or with cotton wool soaked in antiseptic. Only then can the horse be allowed to return to its normal work or grazing.

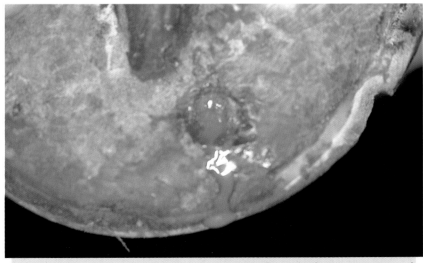

Pus oozing from a puncture wound

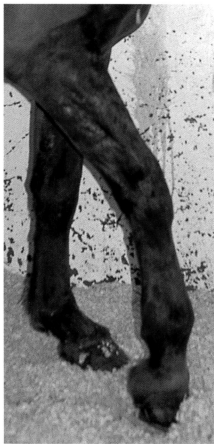

A horse pointing its toe rather than placing any weight on the leg and therefore causing pain. This could indicate a variety of problems associated with the hoof

Symptoms similar to those of **pus** in the foot can occur in a condition known as 'gravel' or white line disease. In this case the infection gains entrance via a defective white line, the structure that links the horizontal sole with the vertical hoof wall.

Treatment: The same as for any pus in the foot.

In other cases an abscess develops in the foot, but even with careful searching of the sole it is not possible to find an entry point. The pus tracks in the direction of least resistance, and this often results in it bursting out at the coronet. The problem in such cases is that gravity will always tend to keep some pus below the coronet. Further **bacterial** multiplication then results in the abscess bursting out again at a later date.

Every effort must be made to provide drainage at the lowest point of the abscess. Care must be taken if poulticing the coronet as the tissues are easily damaged during poulticing, slowing down healing.

In equine terms a corn is an area of bruised horn. The horn swells as it absorbs fluid from the bruising, and the result is very localised pressure on the sensitive structures of the foot. Corns occur in a specific part of the sole known as the seat of corn. In the majority of cases the bruising is caused by an ill-fitting shoe causing pressure on the sole rather than on the wall of the hoof. Another cause is pressure from a **foreign body** such as a stone trapped between the sole and the shoe.

<table>
<tr>
<td>

</td>
<td>

The horse is lame, but the lameness may be intermittent, or it may only be visible when the horse is turning. Pressure from hoof testers will detect the site, and confirmation comes from paring the hoof and seeing the yellowish or reddened horn.

</td>
<td rowspan="2">

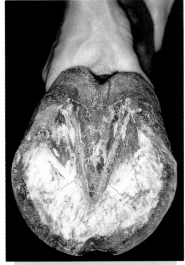

Discoloured horn at the seat of corn

</td>
</tr>
</table>

The shoe should be removed and the discoloured horn cut away. The foot can be either poulticed or tubbed for 48 hours. The foot can then be shod using a shoe that has the ground surface cut away by about a third of its thickness over the affected area. This reduces the pressure on that part of the hoof. Obviously great care must be taken in shoeing the horse subsequently, no matter what the cause.

88 Bruised sole

This term has tended to be used for any traumatic inflammation of the sensitive laminae inside the hoof that does not involve infection. In more recent times tearing or shearing of the laminae has been used as the diagnosis, although as it is not possible to see inside the hoof it is difficult to understand how one can be so exact. The symptoms are a chronic low-grade lameness. The foot may be sensitive to pressure from hoof testers. Sometimes an area of the sole eventually becomes discoloured as a result of absorbing inflammatory fluid.

Rest is essential to allow healing of the sensitive structures. There may be a case for using drugs that improve the circulation within the foot – for example, isoxuprine or acetylpromazine – especially if the **digital pulse** is increased in the affected leg.

89 Ringbone

Ringbone refers to the formation of new bone at the joint between the first and second phalanxes (halfway down the pastern and sometimes called high ringbone) or between the second phalanx and the pedal bone (just below the coronet and sometimes called low ringbone). In carthorses the result could indeed be a visible ring of new bone all around the leg, although often in riding horses there is nothing to see or feel, only new bone visible on an x-ray. In some cases a distinction is made between new bone that is formed away from the joint where the

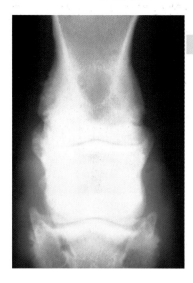

tendon attaches to the bone, and articular ringbone. The cause of ringbone is wear and tear on the structures.

Is it treatable?

Ringbone involving a joint causes permanent lameness that may or may not be improved by the use of painkillers. When the pastern joint is involved, surgical fusion of the joint may resolve the problem, but this is a lengthy process and not free from risk. Non-articular ringbone may settle down in time with rest.

Fetlock lameness 90

The fetlock joint is a complicated structure. There is a relatively straightforward joint between two bones, but there are also two sesamoid bones at the back of the joint, to each of which attaches a branch of the suspensory ligament. On top of that the flexor tendons run through the area. Each of these structures can, and does, develop problems.

What causes it?

The fetlock joint is a common site of OCD in young horses. In older animals degenerative joint disease (DJD) can develop, often originating from a mild OCD lesion that did not cause symptoms in its own right. DJD is the modern description for arthritis that results from wear and tear.

Treatments that may help in the early stages include medication of the joint with hyaluronic acid preparations (replacing the natural joint fluid that loses its lubricating properties in such circumstances); or polysulphated aminoglycosaminoglycan (which protects the joint cartilage); and even **steroids** (which were once thought to cause further deterioration of arthritic joints but which are now widely used to reduce the inflammation). **Anti-inflammatory**, painkilling drugs will have a role to play in enabling the non-competition horse to continue in work: constant, fixed levels of exercise are far more beneficial than resting such horses.

Is it treatable?

A sprain of the branch of the suspensory ligament just above the fetlock joint, or a tear of its attachment to the sesamoid bone, is bad news as the lesions heal very slowly, if at all.

Sprain of suspensory ligament

The sesamoid bones can become inflamed as a result of the stress of exercise, and in this situation are very painful. Diagnosis of sesamoiditis requires x-rays of the bones. Sometimes chip fractures occur from such stressed bones, when surgical removal of the chip is necessary if the horse is to return to soundness.

131

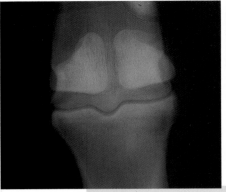
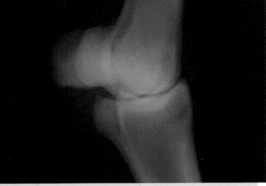

Two x-rays are necessary to get a complete picture of the fetlock joint. On the left the two sesamoid bones can be seen

Is it treatable?

Larger fractures of the sesamoid bones may be repaired surgically: left alone they heal with a fibrous union that will not stand up to fast work.

What to look for

Any inflammation of the fetlock joint is likely to lead to distension of the joint capsule by increased amounts of joint fluid. Because the joint has an annular ligament right around it, the place where the capsule can bulge most easily is behind the leg, just above the sesamoid bones. The result is a large, fluid-filled swelling in exactly the same place as a windgall, the latter being a non-clinical swelling reflecting possibly past joint problems or poor joint conformation. Pressure-bandaging the joint may result in the capsule returning to its normal size.

The annular ligament referred to earlier provides good support to the various structures, but it does have a disadvantage: because it will not readily stretch, if any of the other structures (especially the flexor tendons) becomes thickened, then the pressure on them underneath the annular ligament becomes great. In some such cases the annular ligament has to be cut surgically in order to avoid the pressure causing further damage to the tendon.

91 | Hock lameness

What causes it?

The unusual thing about the hock joint is that although it has half-a-dozen bones, movement only really occurs at one of the joints, that between the tibia and the talus; this is the joint that may show OCD in young horses. It is the other joints, however, thought to have developed to absorb shock, that suffer DJD with wear and tear; such an arthritis is called 'spavin'. In essence, because the small bones are arranged in two layers, there are two possible areas for DJD: between the first and second layers of bone, or between the second layer of bones and the cannon bone. *Treatment*: Spavin causes chronic lameness. If, however, fusion occurs between the two layers of bones, then the pain disappears and the horse becomes sound. This may occur naturally, and initial treatment consists of exercising the horse to promote further new bone growth and hopefully fusion. Painkillers will enable the horse to work without pain. Remedial shoeing, using a lateral extension to the shoe at the heel, helps to encourage the horse to put its foot down properly and so avoid uneven stress on the joints. The lower joint is much more likely to fuse and return to soundness than the upper joint. Surgical or chemical fusion can be carried out.

A major tendon, the superficial flexor tendon, passes over the top of the point of the hock. The ligaments are normally held in place by two small anchoring ligaments. If one or both of these are ruptured, the tendon slips off the top of the *tuber calcaneus* bone, and the joint is then unstable. It may be possible to anchor the tendon surgically.

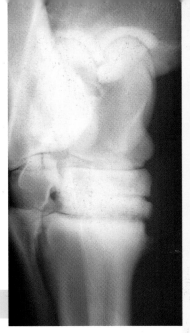

The hock is made up of a large number of bones

Knee lameness 92

The knee is a shock-absorbing joint consisting of a number of bones, but unlike the hock joint in the hind leg, movement is divided more or less evenly between the joints. Behind the joint is a sesamoid bone protecting the flexor tendons. Especially in young horses, a blow to the knee can cause a fracture, perhaps in the form of a slab of bone coming away from one of the bones.

How does it occur?

Surgical repair is the only hope for such knee injuries.

How is it treated?

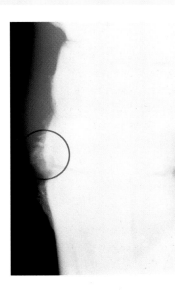

New bone (*circled*) formed on the front of the knee

DJD of the knee 93

This can result in the formation of so much new bone that the joint will not bend properly. **Anti-inflammatory drugs** will at least make movement less painful, even if they do not affect the range of movement possible.

How does it occur?

133

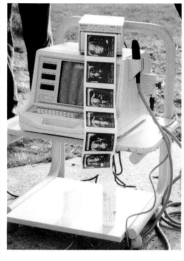

explained

PUS

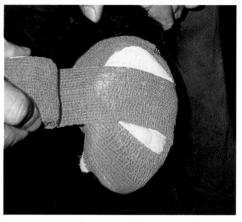

Bandaging a poultice on the sole of a hoof

PUS is a mixture of living and dead bacteria, the inflammatory fluids produced by the body, and the white blood cells that are attracted to the area in order to kill and remove the bacteria.

Not all infections produce pus; it forms when the bacteria remain localised rather than spreading through the body. In certain specialised situations, such as in the guttural pouches or in the foot, the pus may be relatively dry rather than liquid.

Whenever possible pus should be allowed to drain away from the site of its formation. Poulticing may help draw pus out from deeper sites.

ANTIBIOTICS

ANTIBIOTICS are chemical substances that either stop bacteria multiplying (bacteriostats) or kill the bacteria (bacteriocides). Whenever possible, bacteriocidal antibiotics should be used. Antibiotics have no effect at all on viruses.

Unfortunately, as fast as man develops new antibiotics, the bacteria develop resistance to some of the old ones. Where pus is present it is possible to take a swab and culture a minute amount of the infective material in a laboratory. A bacterial sensitivity test then consists of attempting to grow the bacteria in the presence of a range of antibiotics. If the test shows that the bacteria are resistant to an antibiotic, then the drug will not have any clinical value. However, drugs that appear to kill the bacteria in the laboratory will not necessarily do so in real life, where other factors such as the ability of the drug to penetrate to the infection also come into play.

The use of low doses of antibiotics, the frequent changing of antibiotics before the infection has been overcome, and failing to continue antibiotic therapy for a long enough period, all help to encourage the development of antibiotic resistance.

Antibiotics can be administered in three ways: by injection, orally, and topically onto the skin. However, horses are unlike us, for example, in that there are only a couple of antibiotics that are effective when given to them by mouth. Most therefore have to be given by injection.

INJECTIONS

DRUGS CAN BE INJECTED intramuscularly, intravenously, and under the skin. The subcutaneous route is rarely used in the horse because it frequently causes localised reactions. Intravenous injections should really only be given by trained veterinary personnel. The jugular vein in the neck is the one usually used for this.

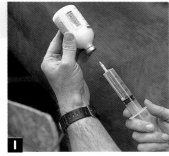

An intramuscular injection has four stages:

1 Fill the syringe. Before the drug can be withdrawn from the bottle, shake the bottle and inject into it the same amount of air as you need to withdraw drug. Then suck out the correct dose into the syringe.

2 Prepare the injection site. Intramuscular injections are usually given into the horse's neck. Imagine the neck divided into three from the head, and draw an imaginary vertical line two-thirds across, then divide it into thirds horizontally and draw a line one-third down. Where the lines cross is the injection site. It is not usually necessary to clip away the hair, but any dirt should be cleaned off, preferably using surgical spirit.

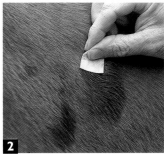

3 Insert the needle. It is not possible to push a needle gently through the horse's skin into the muscle. Hold the needle about 6–12in from the horse, and then with a sudden movement push it right home to the needle hub. Horses react less to the needle insertion if you give the proposed site a few slaps with your hand first. If blood flows out of the needle hub then remove the needle and use a slightly different site.

4 Inject the drug. Attach the syringe firmly to the needle hub and slowly press the plunger fully home. Remove the needle and syringe. Rub the injection site gently if any drug starts to ooze back out from the injection site.

Do not attempt to inject any drug unless you have been trained how to do so and have the necessary sterile needles and syringe. Always dispose of the used ones carefully.

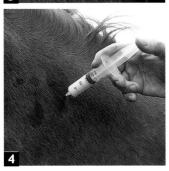

ALLERGY AND HYPERSENSITIVITY

AN ALLERGENIC REACTION occurs when the body uses all or some of its normal responses against noxious substances to react against something that is usually considered harmless. You can never have an allergenic reaction to the first

137

exposure to a substance. However, the more times the body is exposed to contact with the substance, the more likely it is to start to become hypersensitive. Once the body becomes allergic to something it will usually remain so for the rest of its life, even if years go by without any further contact.

Because allergenic reactions involve the production of substances called antibodies either locally or within the bloodstream, it is theoretically possible to confirm what is causing an allergic reaction by detecting those antibodies in the blood. Skin testing by injecting tiny amounts of test substances into the skin in order to see which cause a localised swelling has also been used for this purpose.

Steroids counteract the allergic reaction and so are widely used in the treatment of clinical allergies such as sweet itch or COPD. Because their use may cause side effects it is always preferable to treat allergies by simply preventing any further exposure to the trigger substance.

ANTI-INFLAMMATORY DRUGS

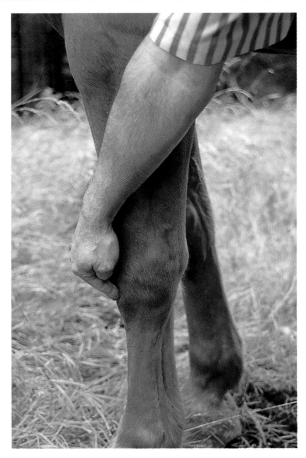

Checking the leg for inflammation

INFLAMMATORY PROCESSES all follow the same pathways. Reaction A triggers off the release of substances B, C and D, which in turn trigger off further reactions until at the bottom of this so-called cascade we see the clinical symptoms. Because pain is part of these reactions (pain and inflammation are always linked), anti-inflammatory drugs also reduce pain; so they may be used as painkillers even though we know they cannot completely remove the inflammation. A case in point is their use to allow a horse to be free from pain despite an ongoing arthritis.

Pain-killing drugs are used in the treatment of colic, where the symptoms we see are the result of inflammatory changes that we cannot see in the bowel wall. One problem that arises here is that if the drug removes the pain we may think that it has also removed the cause of the colic, whereas the internal inflammation continues unseen. Ideally therefore, powerful painkillers should not be used in the treatment of colic until a precise diagnosis has been made, and specific treatment commenced.

The painkillers commonly used in the horse include phenylbutazone (bute), flunixin and vedaprofen. Many of them are available in both oral and injectable formulations. Phenylbutazone is the most commonly used for lameness problems. It has the disadvantage that oral therapy requires 2–3 days before effective tissue levels of the drug are achieved. This compares with vedaprofen where effective levels are achieved within an hour or so. Phenylbutazone can be toxic in small ponies at relatively normal doses. However, it has proved to be quite safe in horses even when used over long periods; hence its use in chronic degenerative joint disease.

STEROIDS

STEROIDS are the body's own anti-inflammatory drug, although many of the drugs we use clinically are modified versions of the natural cortisol molecule. They provide a blanket anti-inflammatory effect without any specific pain-killing effect. So the same drug will stop a horse's beneficial responses to an infection, reduce an allergic reaction, and reduce the inflammation around a burn.

Steroids are powerful drugs that need to be used with care, especially in the following circumstances:
1   They may cause abortion in pregnant mares.
2   Because they reduce a horse's defence mechanisms against infections, they should never be used in the presence of infection unless antibiotic cover is also provided.
3   There have been cases where steroid therapy, especially when given by injection, has been thought to cause laminitis in ponies.

ENDOTOXINS

ENDOTOXINS are poisonous substances formed within bacterial cells, and as such they cause no harm to the horse; it is only when the bacterial cell dies that the endotoxins are released and cause damage. This is in contrast with bacteria such as the Clostridia family, which form exotoxins that are released into their surroundings by the living bacteria. Endotoxins that have been released into the bloodstream can cause damage a considerable distance away from where the parent bacteria lived. An example of this can occur in laminitis, when bacteria in the intestines are killed and their endotoxins released. The endotoxins ultimately cause constriction of the tiny blood vessels in the foot, and so cause laminitis.

PULSE

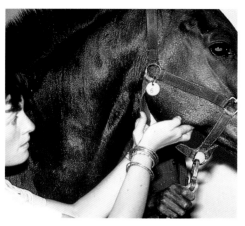

Taking the pulse

THE PULSE is a rhythmic swelling and then contraction of an artery as it pumps blood along. The pulse rate is set by the heart rate, and is identical to it. In the horse we usually take the pulse by placing a forefinger gently on top of the facial artery as it bends over the lower border of the jawbone. You can feel the blood vessel rather like a piece of string between the skin and the jawbone or mandible. Press too hard or too lightly and you cannot feel the pulsations. It takes practice to be able to take a pulse reliably. The normal pulse rate in the horse is around 30–40 per minute.

DIGITAL PULSE

ALL ARTERIES PULSATE, but only where they are relatively exposed between skin and the underlying bone can we feel the pulse.

In the normal horse the digital artery, just behind the bone halfway down the pastern, is too weak to be readily detected.

However, in circumstances where the blood flow through the foot becomes constricted, then the artery has to pulsate harder in an attempt to force the blood through. The pulsation can then be felt and is called a digital pulse. The more obvious the pulsations, the more constricted the blood flow through the foot has become, and this can be used to assess the horse's response to treatment for conditions such as laminitis.

TUMOUR

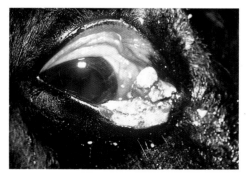

A tumour affecting the eye

THE WORDS 'TUMOUR' AND 'CANCER' are really interchangeable. We use the term 'benign' to describe a tumour that, whilst it may continue growing in size, will not spread to other parts of the body. We use the term 'malignant' to describe a tumour that, whether it grows in size or not, will be very likely to seed further tumours in other parts of the body.

Tumours are collections of cells that have multiplied uncontrollably in numbers, size and even structure. We do not understand why this happens in most cases, nor do we have a means of restoring that control. Instead we usually rely on either removing the whole tumour surgically, or on killing it *in situ* in some way, for example, by using radiation therapy.

ANTISEPTICS AND DISINFECTANTS

THE WORDS 'ANTISEPTIC' AND 'DISINFECTANT' are not interchangeable. An antiseptic is a chemical that can kill bacteria and also usually viruses on the body surface, without in any way damaging the tissues of the body. Antiseptics are not intended to be applied to open wounds. A disinfectant is a chemical that can kill bacteria and viruses, but which may well be toxic to the tissues of the body. So antiseptics are also disinfectants but not vice versa. Disinfectants tend to be more powerful at killing bacteria and viruses than antiseptics, but it is this toxicity that damages cells of the skin if they come into contact with them. Disinfectants and antiseptics always work better if dirt, pus and faeces are cleaned away first. They are used in addition to cleaning, not as a substitute for it, and are often very ineffective cleaning agents. The dilution rate of such powerful chemicals is often crucial to their efficacy. You should dilute liquids as per the manufacturer's directions rather than by emptying an unknown amount of the disinfectant into a bucket of water.

BLOOD ENZYMES

CHEMICALS CALLED ENZYMES are vital to body functions, and are involved in all the metabolic processes that make life possible. Some enzymes are present throughout the body, but others may only be present in one or more particular tissues such as muscle or liver. Because living cells are constantly dying and being replaced, there is a constant low level of such enzymes being released into the bloodstream. We can measure these enzyme levels and arrive at normal levels for the healthy horse population, or even better, for an individual horse. When a tissue is damaged by injury or disease, increased amounts of the enzymes found there will be released into the bloodstream. Blood sampling will detect this, and warn us that tissue damage has occurred. We can also take a number of blood samples over a period of time and see whether the damage is getting worse or better.

Blood enzyme levels are particularly valuable for warning us about internal problems, such as liver disease, and problems that may have non-specific symptoms, such as low-grade azoturia.

The samples should be treated carefully between collection and the analysis; ideally they should be kept refrigerated. Analysis should be carried out as soon as possible, because the enzyme levels can change even after the blood has been removed from the body.

ALBUMEN AND GLOBULIN

THE PROTEINS IN THE BLOOD are of two main sorts: albumen and globulin. The albumens are the structural proteins, and have a vital role in keeping water molecules inside the blood vessels. A low albumen level will allow fluid to seep out through the blood vessel walls into the surrounding tissues. So if the bowel wall is damaged and protein is being lost via that route, the horse will often develop oedema of the legs or brisket associated with those low protein levels. A blood sample will enable us to distinguish between oedema due to a local problem, and oedema associated with low protein levels in the body as a whole.

Globulins are the proteins of the immune system; thus antibodies against infection are globulins. If a foal has low globulin levels during its first week of life, it means that it has not absorbed vital antibodies from its mother's first milk, or colostrum, and that foal will be significantly more susceptible to infection than one that had normal globulin levels. Furthermore, statistics show that this susceptibility will continue for many months.

A high globulin level in a horse's blood probably indicates that it is fighting an infection of some sort. This response applies to some internal parasites as well as to bacteria or viruses. Raised levels of one of the globulins provide a vital confirmation that strongyle worm larvae are present in the body in large numbers.

Sensitive analytical techniques enable us to measure the antibody globulins against a specific disease. The standard method of confirming that a horse has had an infection with a particular respiratory virus, for example, is to take two blood samples 14 days apart, and to measure antibody levels. If there has been active infection, then the levels will have increased rapidly during that time. This is a particularly useful technique because it may not be possible to isolate the virus or bacterium itself.

DIURETICS

DIURETICS are drugs that act on the kidney to increase the amount of urine produced. This is surprisingly useful. It can, for example, reduce the amount of oedema around a wound by drawing fluid out of the blood at the kidney, fluid which is then replaced by fluid re-entering the bloodstream from the oedematous area. Similarly the use of diuretics may reduce congestion in the lungs during heart disease.

Frusemide is the drug most commonly used as a diuretic in the horse. In certain American states it is legitimate to race horses that are receiving frusemide. It is used to reduce the incidence of exercise-induced pulmonary haemorrhage. Unfortunately the use of diuretics can also make the detection of other drugs, such as painkillers, more difficult; which is why, in most competitions in the rest of the world, the use of diuretics is banned.

ELECTROLYTES

ELECTROLYTES are certain electrically charged chemical elements that are basic to life. Very simply, sodium chloride is just salt, but sodium+ and chloride- separately are both electrolytes. The most important electrolytes are sodium, potassium, chloride and bicarbonate. They play a vital role in allowing substances to pass through the individual cell wall membranes.

Muscles cannot contract if the electrolyte balance of the cells and the surrounding tissue fluid is not correct. When a horse sweats it loses electrolytes in the sweat, and this means that its muscle activity becomes temporarily compromised. So electrolyte supplements are often given to horses taking part in activities such as endurance rides where they will sweat considerably. When a horse has diarrhoea it loses electrolytes and its muscles become weak because they cannot work properly without those electrolytes.

We can measure blood electrolyte levels, but it is important to appreciate that these levels change frequently and should be interpreted accordingly. Thus a blood sodium level taken yesterday may have little significance for today.

Electrolytes lost through sweat can be replaced with supplements

CAPILLARY REFILL TIME

MEASURING THE CAPILLARY REFILL TIME is a simple test of circulatory function that anyone can perform. Using a finger or thumb, you exert firm pressure on a pink area of the horse's gums for a few seconds. When you remove the finger, the place where you pressed will be white. You then count the time taken for the

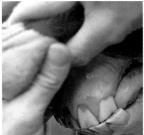

After pressing on the gum (left), the capillary refill time is then measured as the pink colour returns (right)

normal pink colour to return. A capillary refill time of 4sec or less is normal.

Surveys have shown that in acute colic, for example, the single most reliable way to forecast whether the horse will recover is to monitor its capillary refill time.

RECTAL EXAMINATION

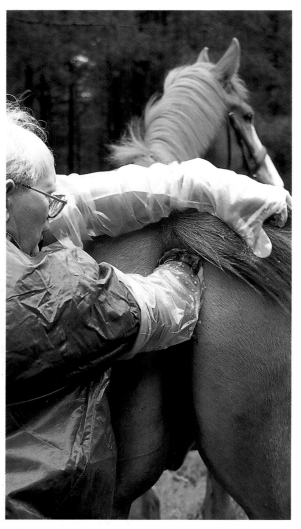

Rectal examination requires care for the safety of both horse and vet

A RECTAL EXAMINATION is generally carried out for one of two possible reasons: to examine the reproductive system; and to assess the digestive system during colic. It requires considerable skill to carry out the examination, because the rectal wall in the horse is very fragile, and rupturing it during an unskilled examination can be fatal for the horse.

The amount of information that can be obtained during a rectal examination depends on the size and temperament of the horse, and perhaps also on the size of the vet's arm! We can normally feel both ovaries and the uterus, although during pregnancy this can sink down to the floor of the abdomen, out of reach. We can feel part of the colon, the caecum, and the relative positions of much of the digestive system, but not the stomach and other parts of the anterior abdomen.

Carrying out a rectal examination can be very dangerous for the vet because the horse can kick out without warning. It is often therefore carried out over a stable door or with the horse restrained in stocks.

EUTHANASIA

THE DECISION TO END A HORSE'S LIFE is never taken lightly. It might be that old age means that he no longer has an acceptable quality of life; or perhaps he has an incurable condition that is causing him significant pain.

Traditionally euthanasia of the horse involved shooting it with a specially adapted handgun that fires a bullet, or with a captive bolt pistol. The loud noise may distress people, but the effect is instantaneous: the horse falls to the ground and stops breathing, the heartbeat stopping soon afterwards.

In recent times owners have increasingly asked that euthanasia should be carried out using an overdose of barbiturate injected into the jugular vein. This requires the injection of a relatively large volume of fluid, and the injection may need to be continued after the horse has collapsed to the ground. Incorporating cinchocaine into the injection reduces the amount of gasping for air that might otherwise occur.

The disposal of a dead horse may pose considerable problems. If the local hunt kennels or abattoir service cannot take the body, the options are cremation or burial. Cremation is expensive, but it may be the only alternative for owners who do not have the facilities for burial. If the body is to be buried, care must be taken to choose a site well away from any drainage ditch or water course. Horses euthanased by injection cannot be used for meat, even for animal feed.

TEETH RASPING

A TOOTH RASP is really a file on a long handle. The rasping surface may involve forming the metal head into many cutting edges, or it may be made by embedding a hard material such as tungsten carbide into a holding material. The rasp is moved in and out along the line of the horse's molar, or cheek teeth. The rasping surface is held at an angle to reflect the fact that it is the outer edge of the upper molars and the inner edge of the lower molars that generally become sharp. The rasp needs frequent cleaning in water to prevent the cutting edges becoming clogged by tooth material. Electric tooth rasps are available, though their weight and noise during use may upset some horses.

Effective rasping of the teeth can only be done when the horse's jaws are wide enough apart for the rasp to move freely. This is rarely possible without the use of some form of gag to prevent the mouth closing.

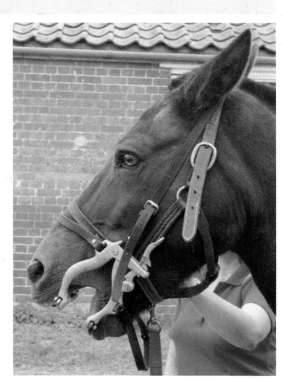

A Houseman gag holds a horse's mouth open to allow a detailed dental examination to take place

ENDOSCOPY

The flexible endoscope inserted through a nostril and down the respiratory system produces a video image on the screen

THIS TECHNIQUE usually involves using a bundle of flexible glass fibres to look inside the body. Originally it was the respiratory system that was investigated in this way, enabling the vet to examine all the way from the nostrils down to the entrance to the lungs. Endoscopes are also used to investigate the digestive system, passing down the oesophagus into the stomach. An arthroscope is a specialist kind of endoscope that is used for looking inside joints.

The endoscope consists of a powerful light source that is transmitted down one set of the fibres. The illuminated object is then viewed through a lens via another set of fibres. The outer flexible endoscopic tube also incorporates hollow channels that can be used to carry water or to remove fluids, and to enable tiny instruments to be inserted into the area that is being investigated. In the case of arthroscopy in particular there is a wide range of miniature power tools that can be manipulated in this way.

Video endoscopes or arthroscopes show the image on a screen, enlarged many times, rather than the vet having to hold the instrument up to their eye.

RADIOGRAPHY

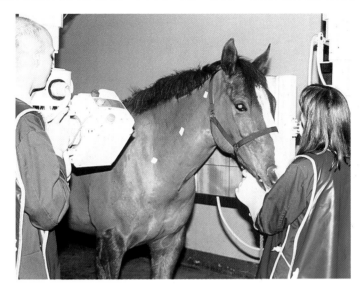

Damage to a shoulder could be muscle-related, but radiography is able to detect whether or not it is something more serious, such as a bone fracture

RADIOGRAPHY was the first technique that let us look inside the body without surgery. It works by means of a beam of x-rays from the machine passes through the target and hits an x-ray plate. The film inside then has to be developed in a dark room, although in many cases the actual developing process is carried out automatically. The x-ray image is black, white and all the shades of grey. It records density rather than structure, so bone can be seen in great detail but muscles only show as an amorphous grey. Nevertheless a skilled radiographer can obtain a considerable amount of information about structures other than bone. Cartilage does not show on x-ray at all, however, which means that many arthritic changes do not show, either.

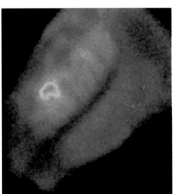

The horse's leg up to the knee and hock can be radiographed very well with mobile machines, but the rest of the body may need more powerful, fixed machines – and even then, the thickest part of the body, such as the spine, can be difficult to radiograph perfectly.

As when we take an ordinary photograph, the exposure used makes a big difference to the quality of the final x-ray. Vets can vary the kilovoltage that is used to generate the x-rays, affecting their penetration, and also the milliamperage, affecting the contrast of the image. There are now also digital x-ray machines that can alter the image electronically, at will.

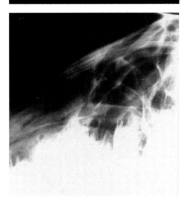

Scintigraphy (top) and radiography can provide invaluable information about dental problems

ULTRASOUND

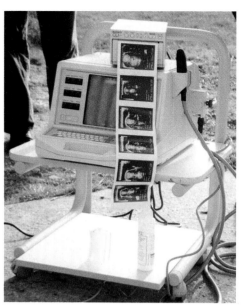

Ultrasound scans are invaluable when examination of delicate tissues and organs is necessary, eg during pregnancy

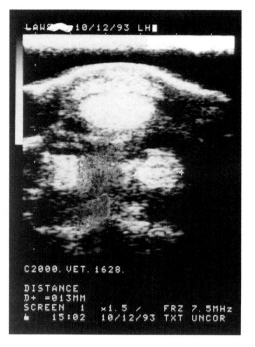

Ultrasound image of a horse's tendons. The skin is at the top and the bone is at the bottom

ULTRASOUND scan pictures are black and white images like x-rays, but they show us different information. Thus a scan shows a cross-sectional picture, a slice across rather than a normal picture. The image is viewed on a screen, but a print of the image can also be made. The scan shows soft tissues such as skin, tendons, the uterus or the heart, but the ultrasound beam is reflected by bone, and anything behind a bone surface is invisible. Air also reflects the beam.

When scanning, the quality of the image depends very much on the degree of contact between the ultrasound head and the surface of the body. Hair makes skin contact poor when scanning tendons, for example, and it is customary to clip off the hair and apply a contact gel to remedy this.

Doppler ultrasound measures the flow rates of fluids, and so is used to evaluate the heart and other major blood vessels. Colours are used to differentiate the different velocities of fluid flow, and the movements of the heart chambers, valves and so on, are shown as they happen, like a movie rather than a still photograph.

Ultrasound images are particularly useful for assessing the improvement or deterioration of a problem. Being non-invasive and non-painful we can carry out repeated scans over time without any risk to either horse or handlers.

HEART-BAR SHOE

THE HEART-BAR SHOE is used to provide the same direct support for the bony column of the foot and pastern as it does for the hoof wall. It does this by means of a V-shaped insert that follows the contours of the frog. When fitting the shoe, care must be taken that it does not extend outside the frog outline and press on the sole; nor must the insert be angled upwards too much so that at rest it is pressing into the frog. Fitted badly the shoe can cause increased pain, rather than reducing it. The shoe's most common application is in laminitis.

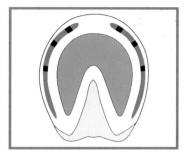

The insert is shaped to follow the contours of the frog

FROG PAD

A FROG PAD fulfils a similar function to a heart-bar shoe, but it can be applied by the horse owner and it does not run the risk of causing additional pain. It is possible to buy rubber frog pads that only require trimming to the shape of the frog before being bandaged in place. They are very effective. In an emergency, the do-it-yourself version is a firm roll of bandage placed over the frog and secured by bandaging.

BITLESS BRIDLE

ORIGINALLY A BITLESS BRIDLE was used when a horse greatly resented the presence of the bit in its mouth, perhaps because for one reason or another it caused discomfort and pain. More recently it has been claimed that the use of an orthodox bridle causes the horse to flex its head towards its chest even with the best of riders, and that this significantly reduces the airway at the larynx.

Bitless bridles such as the Spirit bridle have been suggested to help in a number of possible laryngeal problems, including tongue swallowing, head shaking and EIPH.

At first riders may be concerned that they will not have sufficient control over the horse without a bit, but the earlier hackamoor bitless bridle was always thought of as a means to control a horse that was uncontrollable in a normal bridle.

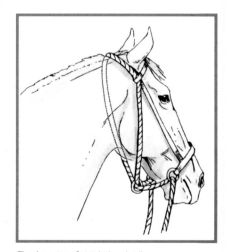

The American Spirit bitless bridle

SHAMPOOING A HORSE

'Thatching', placing straw under a sweat rug, will allow a wet horse to dry without becoming chilled

SHAMPOOING A HORSE is basically just the same as washing our own hair: wet the coat, apply the shampoo to make a lather all over, and then rinse with clean water. It is the aftercare that is important.

After rinsing, use a sweat scraper to remove the excess water from the neck, body and upper legs. Dry the pasterns and heels carefully with a towel in order to avoid mud fever, and then slowly walk the horse in hand until it is dry. Then put on a sweat rug. In very cold weather a layer of straw under the sweat rug will provide thermal insulation whilst still allowing evaporation.

BLOOD SAMPLING

BLOOD SAMPLES are usually taken from the jugular vein that runs along the horse's neck a couple of inches up from its lower border. The amount of blood removed varies depending on the tests required. Thus a blood sample to detect drugs – for instance, testing for painkillers at the time of purchase or during a competition – requires a relatively large amount, whereas taking blood to examine just the blood cells it contains will only require a very small volume.

Once the sample has been obtained, it is important that it is correctly identified, and then it must be stored correctly. The sample may need to be divided into two or three parts in order to mix it with different coagulants prior to analysis. The shorter the period of storage the more accurate the results are likely to be.

STOMACH TUBE

A STOMACH TUBE is a flexible hollow tube made out of either rubber or polythene. One end is rounded so that it does not damage sensitive structures whilst it is being inserted, and the other end may be adapted so that it can easily be attached to a stomach pump. The tube is inserted into a nostril and guided into the passageway that leads into the pharynx at the back of the mouth. Horses may resent it being passed along the first couple of inches but after this they usually do not object. When the end of the tube reaches the larynx the vet has to gently persuade the horse to 'swallow' the tube so that it goes into the oesophagus rather than into the trachea, or windpipe. This stage of the operation can require great patience in some horses. The tube can then be pushed along the length of the oesophagus and into the stomach.

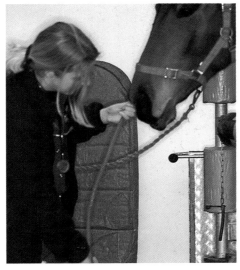

The stomach tube is inserted via a nostril to avoid it being bitten if passed down via the mouth

Sometimes a stomach tube is used in order to put liquids into the horse's stomach: for example, liquid paraffin for a horse that has an impaction colic. Sometimes it is used to flush in water and then suck it out again in an attempt to remove the material blocking the oesophagus when the horse has choked.

Care must be taken when removing the stomach tube to prevent the end damaging the sensitive structures in the pharynx and nasal chambers.

NEBULISATION

IT IS OFTEN DESIRABLE TO TARGET A DRUG at the specific part of the body where its effect is needed. One of the few instances where this is actually possible is for the lungs: by mixing a drug with the air a horse breathes we can be sure that it will go directly into the lungs. There are practical difficulties, however, in that the liquid or powder that needs to be given has to have just the right particle size to ensure that it will remain suspended in the air right down into the alveoli, or air sacs, in the lung, and

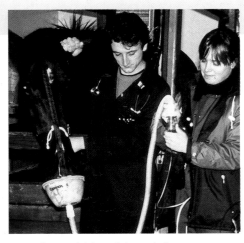

Drugs administered via a nebuliser

not be deposited in the nasal passages, for example, where its effect will be negligible.

A nebuliser ensures that only particles of a specific microscopic size will be mixed with the air drawn through the apparatus, and that they will be evenly dispersed. Human nebulisers are not suitable for horses, and equine nebulisers have to cope with large volumes of air breathed in by the horse, even at rest.

COPD is the most common condition treated by nebulisation.

DOPPLER ULTRASOUND

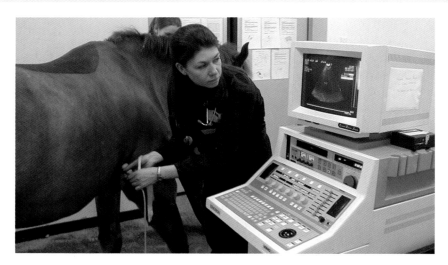

The ultrasound beam has to be directed between the horse's ribs

TECHNIQUES SUCH AS RADIOGROPHY and ultrasound are really intended to reveal the body's internal structures. Doppler ultrasound is not so much concerned with structure, as with function.

Utilisation of the doppler principle enables us to measure the flow of a liquid along a tube, and doppler ultrasound enables us to measure the rate of flow through internal structures. The most common use of doppler ultrasound is to measure the rate of flow of blood through the heart and associated large blood vessels. The ultimate refinement is to have the different flow rates displayed as different colours, so that the operator can focus on a particular heart valve or blood vessel and see at a glance whether the blood flow rate is uniform and normal.

Doppler ultrasound is particularly useful in the evaluation of the significance of heart murmurs and arrhythmias. These can sound very abnormal, but if their effect on blood flow is limited, then their effect on the horse's performance will also be minimal. In the past the high incidence of heart murmurs in the horse has led to horses being quite wrongly considered unsuitable for strenuous exercise, whereas the use of doppler ultrasound on the horse whilst working on a treadmill might show that the murmur had no significant effect even at speed.

VACCINATION

THE TERMS 'VACCINATION' AND 'INNOCULATION' are technically different, but for practical purposes they are interchangeable. Vaccination is the process by which a foreign substance is introduced into the horse in order to stimulate it to produce immunity, or protection, against a specific infectious disease. Sometimes that immunity takes the form of producing large quantities of antibodies in the blood that can counter the infection. Such antibodies can be measured in a blood sample. Sometimes the immunity takes the form of local antibodies, and although they provide just as effective a degree of protection against the disease, they may not be readily measured.

The ideal vaccine has the following properties:

a) It is safe to use in the horse and does not cause reactions around the injection site.
b) Its use does not affect other horses with which it may come into contact.
c) It is effective at killing the disease organism in the horse before it can cause disease.
d) It is effective at preventing the disease organism spreading to other horses after infection.
e) It is not expensive.

Vaccines often contain a substance called an adjuvant that increases the reaction of the tissues to the vaccine itself and so increases the immunity produced. Unfortunately it is often the case that the more effective the adjuvant is at doing this, the more likely it is to produce a significant localised reaction in the horse. In some cases this may just take the form of a small amount of swelling that disappears within a day or so; in others the area may become hot and painful, and produce a form of sterile abscess. Even so, just because a horse has a localised reaction to one dose of vaccine, it does not mean that it will react in the same way to future doses. Owners have blamed vaccination for a loss of performance in the days or weeks following the injection, but scientific analysis of large numbers of vaccinated and non-vaccinated horses has so far failed to support this.

The aim of vaccination is obviously to prevent the horse suffering any disease symptoms should it come into contact with that particular disease in the future (vaccines do not have any effect if the horse already has the disease). It is a significant point that some vaccines will do this, but will not prevent the disease organism establishing itself in the horse's body. Such a horse can then shed the organism into the environment, or it can infect other unvaccinated horses, even though it remains free of symptoms itself. When choosing a vaccine it is therefore desirable to use one where such shedding does not occur. Currently there is considerable interest in aerosol vaccines against respiratory disease. Such a vaccine stimulates both the anatomical area and the type of immunity that would be responsible for natural immunity. It also looks as if surface-acting vaccines may produce immunity far stronger than is obtained with injectable vaccination.

Vaccines are never 100 per cent effective, and there are always some horses that do not respond. It is generally accepted that approximately 80 per cent of a group of horses needs to have been vaccinated in order to prevent an epidemic of the disease in those horses.

Vaccines can be manufactured in a variety of ways. They may contain live organisms that have been modified in some way to prevent them causing disease whilst still allowing them to stimulate immunity. Vaccines may contain whole dead organisms, or only specific groups of molecules from the organism. They may contain a different organism that has been genetically modified so that it contains just the portion of the disease organism that stimulates most immunity. Vaccines may not produce immunity against the disease organism at all, but against the toxin that it produces, and which causes the symptoms.

The frequency at which a vaccine needs to be given varies from one to another. Generally, live vaccines need only one initial dose, but dead vaccines require two doses, separated by a month; all equine vaccines then require booster doses. Most commonly these are at yearly intervals, but some virus vaccines require more frequent boosting. When the regulators of equine events or government bodies involved in the transport of horses decide upon minimum vaccination requirements against a disease, these are not necessarily the same as the manufacturers' recommendations. The internationally recognised minimum vaccination programme against equine influenza, for example, stipulates vaccination at different times to the manufacturers of some of the vaccines on the market. You should consider the manufacturers' recommendations to be the absolute minimum.

It is important to keep an accurate record of all vaccinations given to your horse, signed by the vet concerned, as you may be required to produce it to gain entry to an event. Moreover it can be difficult – or well nigh impossible – to provide duplicate certificates, so guard the documentation carefully.

PRESSURE PADS

PRESSURE ON A bleeding wound is a quick, readily available and effective way to stop all but the most severe bleeding. A pad is held firmly against the wound until the bleeding stops. A clean handkerchief or a folded piece of gamgee or bandage make good pads. Cotton wool is less effective because the strands pull too much of the clot away when you lift the pad off. For this reason it is always preferable to put a non-stick dressing under the pad if one is available. Resist the temptation to keep checking to see if the bleeding has stopped – give the clot a chance to form properly first.

TEMPERATURE

WHEN WE SPEAK OF A HORSE'S TEMPERATURE we are not referring to its surface temperature, but of the temperature of its inner tissues and organs. The average temperature for a healthy horse is 101–101.5°F or 38.5°C. Very strenuous exercise, excitement or pain may all produce a higher temperature. Compared with some other species of animals the horse's temperature does not increase greatly as a result of the presence of infection. Any temperature higher than 103° should be treated very seriously indeed.

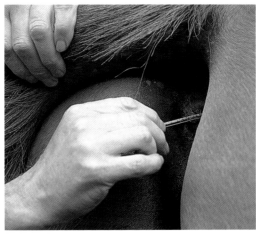

Once the thermometer is inserted into the rectum, do not let go of it

There are two types of clinical thermometer: mercury and digital. The electronic thermometers do cost more than the mercury ones, but they withstand dropping on the stable floor much better! The thermometer is inserted, bulb end first, into the horse's rectum for approximately 75 per cent of its length; be careful to keep hold of the end of the thermometer, because there is always the risk of it being sucked right inside, or flicked away by the tail. The temperature is read after a minute. Mercury thermometers are difficult to read, and owners should practise to make sure that they can read one quickly and accurately. Always reset the thermometer after use either by shaking the mercury down, or by resetting the electronic version. Do not take a horse's temperature immediately after it has passed faeces, as this may give a false reading.

BRONCHODILATORS

BRONCHODILATORS are drugs that open previously constricted bronchioles in the lungs and thus increase airflow in and out of the alveoli where oxygen exchange actually takes place. They have little or no effect on healthy lungs at exercise – they cannot increase the diameter beyond normality. Their action is achieved by selectively stimulating the tiny muscles that dilate the airway, rather than those that constrict it. Clenbuterol is the most widely used bronchodilator, and is commonly used in the treatment of COPD and similar conditions.

The ability to increase the diameter of small tubes through which air flows also extends to tubes through which blood flows; thus bronchodilators may increase the blood supply to the foot. One side effect is that they may cause patchy sweating. They should not be used in late pregnancy.

INTRAVENOUS FLUIDS

HORSES LOSE FLUID from their general circulation for a variety of reasons, including haemorrhage, diarrhoea, sweating, dehydration and shock. It is possible to replace that fluid by putting a flexible tube into a major vein and allowing fluid to run into the vein under the force of gravity. Horses are large animals and so require large volumes of fluid; 5l would be a common starting dose. The rate of administration is also important: thus 5l over twenty-four hours would not have as much effect as 5l given over one hour.

Water stays in the blood because it is held there by the concentration of salts called electrolytes. Without them it would seep through the blood vessel wall and out into the tissues by the process of osmosis. So giving just water intravenously would only have a very temporary effect before it disappeared. We have to give a mixture of water and electrolytes so that the fluid will remain in the circulation long enough to do some good. For this, a variety of electrolyte solutions is used, including saline (which includes ordinary salt) and lactated Ringers solution (which contains sodium lactate, sodium chloride, potassium chloride and also calcium chloride).

The fluid given needs to be sterile, so that it doesn't introduce infection, and it should be at or around body heat, so that it does not cause small blood vessels to constrict in reaction to the cold.

There are occasions when fluids containing abnormally high concentrations of electrolytes are used in order to draw fluid into the bloodstream from the surrounding tissues. This fluid is called hypertonic saline. When whole blood has been lost as a result of a major haemorrhage, then whole blood may be the ideal intravenous fluid.

TOXOIDS AND ANTI-TOXINS

A NUMBER OF BACTERIA, especially from the Clostridia family, cause disease by releasing a poisonous toxin into the body. In these cases, killing the bacteria will not stop the symptoms, because the toxin is still present. Nevertheless, specific anti-toxins may be available to block the effect of the toxin. The most common anti-toxin available for use in horses is tetanus anti-toxin. This can be injected as soon as the risk of exposure to tetanus is known, and will usually prevent the development of symptoms. It may also counteract clinical symptoms after they have developed, and so treat clinical cases of tetanus. The protection provided by anti-toxin only lasts for about three weeks.

A toxoid is a special type of vaccine that stimulates the horse to make anti-toxin rather than antibodies against the bacteria. Producing full protection by the use of a toxoid will always be preferable to hoping that you will become aware of the need to give a dose of anti-toxin before it is too late.

DEHYDRATION

IN THE HEALTHY HORSE there is a balance between the fluid in the tissues and that in the blood. If fluid is lost from the tissues, then more will flow into them from the blood. This in turn means that there will be less fluid in the blood than there should be. The number of blood cells will not have changed, but they will represent a higher percentage of the blood's volume, and the blood will be thicker, or more viscous. It will thus take more effort to pump it around the body. This situation is called dehydration.

Dehydration can occur as a result of hot climate, sweating, lack of adequate drinking water or diarrhoea. The deficiency may be of either water or of the electrolytes which hold that water in the blood by osmotic pressure. Early stages of dehydration can only be diagnosed from a blood sample, which reveals that the Packed Cell Volume (PCV) is high. When 10-15% of the tissue fluid has been lost the skin loses its normal elasticity. As a result when you pick up a fold on the horse's neck and then release it, the fold does not immediately disappear, but remains for several seconds before slowly flattening out. By the time you find that this amount of fluid has been lost, veterinary help should be obtained.

The horse's natural response to dehydration is to drink more water, but if it is severely dehydrated it may become depressed and will either stop drinking altogether, or drink less than it requires. Intravenous fluids may then be necessary.

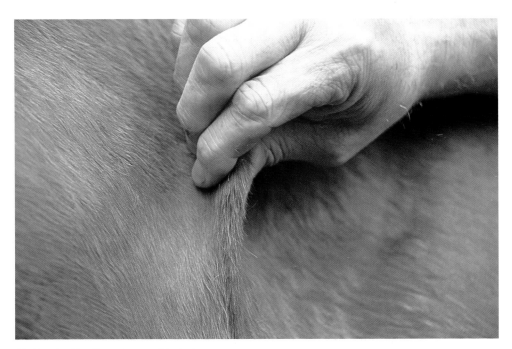

Pinching the skin will reveal severe dehydration

DRUG RESISTANCE

A DISTINCTION has to be made between drug resistance and drug tolerance. Drug resistance only really occurs in respect of antibiotics, when bacteria develop the ability to resist the effects of that antibiotic. Drug tolerance can occur in a number of classes of drugs and reflects a situation where higher and higher doses of the drug are needed to produce the same clinical effect. Drug tolerance may sometimes only reflect the fact that the clinical situation is deteriorating: more pain may require more painkiller.

There are very few antibiotics to which bacteria have never developed resistance, and these drugs tend to be reserved for emergency use in human beings. Vets aim to select an antibiotic to which the infection present probably will not be resistant, but only if they first culture the bacteria in a laboratory and then test to see which antibiotics kill off the bacteria there ('*in vitro*' as it is called) can they really be sure that the choice is the right one. Even then the antibiotic may not work in the clinical situation (or '*in vivo*') because of factors such as a failure on the part of the drug to penetrate through the inflamed tissues to the source of the infection.

Antibiotic resistance can be infectious between bacteria. So if bacteria A develops resistance to antibiotic X, it can pass that resistance on to bacteria B. Antibiotic resistance is encouraged by:

a) using low doses of antibiotics;
b) stopping treatment too soon, before all the bacteria have been killed;
c) changing the antibiotic frequently;
d) using an antibiotic which only stops the bacteria multiplying (a bacteriostatic antibiotic) rather than one that actually kills them (a bacteriocidal antibiotic).

Drug resistance is long lasting, and clinical records have an important part to play in guiding a vet's choice of drugs on a particular premises.

GLUCOSE TOLERANCE TEST

THIS TEST consists of giving a large amount of glucose solution directly into the horse's stomach via a stomach tube, having first starved the horse for 12 hours. Blood samples are then taken hourly and the blood glucose levels measured.

In a horse that is absorbing nutrients normally, the blood glucose level will double within two hours before dropping back to its original level. Horses that are not absorbing nutrients properly will show little or no rise in blood glucose levels.

The test is most commonly carried out on horses that are losing weight despite eating well, in order to decide if their food is being absorbed into the body or not.

ADMINISTERING MEDICINE IN PASTE FORM

PASTES are a convenient and reliable way to give medicines such as wormers, painkillers or antibiotics.

1   Estimate the horse's weight accurately, using a weight tape if one is available. Then preset the correct dose in the syringe.

2   Holding the horse's head up with one hand by the lead rope, insert the syringe through the corner of the lips so that the nozzle lies on the back of the tongue.

3   Press the plunger fully home. Remove the syringe from the horse's mouth, twisting it as you do so to dislodge any paste still attached.

4   Keep the horse's head raised until you are happy that the paste has been swallowed. Dispose of the empty syringe carefully.

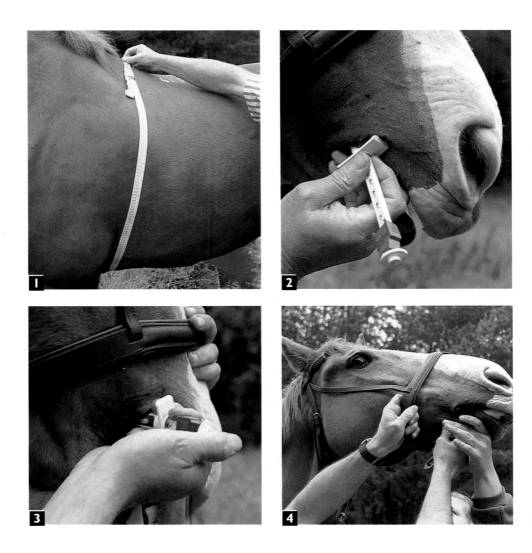

BIOPSY

A BIOPSY is a small piece of tissue taken from the living animal for future examination under a microscope. The actual amount of tissue removed varies tremendously depending on the circumstances. The sample must be placed in a preservative solution immediately after collection in order to prevent any post-mortem changes developing. Probably the most common reason for carrying out a biopsy is to find out whether a tumour is present, and if so, to establish whether it is malignant or not.

Using ultrasound it may be possible to guide a biopsy 'punch' very precisely into a target area in even an internal organ such as the liver.

NERVE BLOCKS

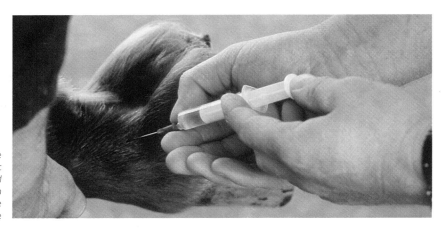

A small volume of anaesthetic being placed around an appropriate nerve

A NERVE BLOCK is a means of temporarily removing all sensation from a specific part of the body. It is commonly used in the diagnosis of lameness, when the vet is looking to see whether the lameness is significantly reduced if sensation is removed from a particular part of the leg or foot. A positive nerve block is one where removal of sensation produces an improvement in the horse's condition.

The technique consists of injecting a small volume of local anaesthetic directly around a nerve. It may take up to twenty minutes for the drug to be absorbed into the nerve, and for it to stop pain impulses travelling past that point. The duration of action is variable, but several hours must elapse before the nerve can be considered to be transmitting impulses normally again. A slight inflammatory swelling may occur after the injection.

The common sites for nerve blocks are shown in the diagram. When trying to pinpoint lameness, the first principle is to carry out the lowest nerve block first. The vet must also remember that if he blocks a large area as a kind of screening measure, and the block is positive, then it will be some time before he can try more narrowly targeted nerve blocks.

Occasionally a nerve block gives a false negative result. This may occur because that individual horse has a slightly different neurological anatomy, or perhaps because for some reason it has not been possible to inject the local anaesthetic directly alongside the nerve.

Nerve blocks do not give false positive results – unlike a very similar technique, where the local anaesthetic is injected into a joint rather than around a nerve, and which may give a false positive. This is because in some circumstances joint cavities link up with other structures. For example, injecting local anaesthetic into the distal inter-digital, or coffin joint, may cause a horse with navicular disease to go sound because the navicular bursa has an opening into the coffin joint and the local anaesthetic can travel through this. It sometimes happens that a nerve block of an area is positive, but no cause of the lameness can be found in that area even though there are, for example, x-ray changes elsewhere. In these circumstances we should always believe the nerve block rather than the x-ray or the scintigraphy, because only the nerve block tells us about the pain a horse is feeling and which is causing the lameness.

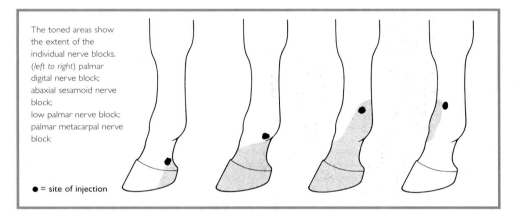

The toned areas show the extent of the individual nerve blocks. (*left to right*) palmar digital nerve block; abaxial sesamoid nerve block; low palmar nerve block; palmar metacarpal nerve block

● = site of injection

FOOT BALANCE

EVERY TIME that a horse puts its foot to the ground, percussion forces travel right up the leg. Any variation in the shape of the hoof alters these forces and increases or decreases the likelihood of lameness occurring because of abnormal stresses. With a properly balanced foot the stresses are minimal: but what constitutes a balanced foot?

Firstly, the front wall of the hoof should be parallel with an imaginary line drawn down the centre of the pastern. If the toe is too long these two lines will converge, and the weight of the horse will be thrown towards the heel rather than the centre of the hoof. If the toe is too short the two lines will diverge and the weight will be thrown towards the toe.

Secondly, the sides of the hoof should both be of equal length and at the same angle to the vertical. If they are not, the forces will be greater up one side of the leg than up the other.

Finally, when we look at the sole of the foot, a line drawn from the middle of the toe to the corner of the heel should be exactly the same length as a line drawn across the widest part of the foot.

Left to their own devices the majority of wild horses have quite well balanced feet. The problem is that we like to interfere. We keep horses on soft ground so that the hoof isn't worn down, or we exercise them on hard surfaces so that the hoof is worn down excessively. And as if that is not enough, we fit shoes, thus stopping any natural wear at all and, more importantly, inflicting on the horse the shape of hoof the farrier happened to give him when he trimmed him, for good or ill. There are even fashions of foot balancing that are claimed to be better for the horse, but which all too often make things worse, especially in inexperienced hands.

LASER THERAPY

Laser treatment applied to the tendon of a foreleg

A LASER is a machine that emits light of one specific wavelength in a parallel beam. Therapeutic lasers are sometimes said to be either hot or cold: hot lasers are surgical lasers that can cut and remove tissue very precisely; cold lasers do not cause any tissue damage (except perhaps if pointed directly at the sensitive retina of the eye). They have a variety of effects on the tissues that are exposed to them, but whatever the localised effects, there is also some effect on the body as a whole. Certain anti-inflammatory substances produced by the body, such as cortisol and others, are significantly increased in the blood after laser treatment. The levels reach a peak about four hours after treatment, and remain raised for about four days.

Lasers are used to reduce inflammation, especially the inflammatory processes that cause swelling. So they are used to reduce the swelling associated with an acutely sprained tendon, for example – although it must be appreciated that just because the swelling goes down, it does not mean that the tendon itself is necessarily healed. Lasers are used to speed up wound healing. They can do this in fresh, sutured wounds, but are more commonly used in open wounds where new skin cells have to grow in from the edges of the wound. Lasers can also relieve pain, and this appears to occur through a mechanism similar to acupuncture. Thus directing a laser at an acupuncture site along the back can reduce painful muscle spasm.

Although the clinical effects of laser therapy can easily be demonstrated, the mechanism by which that effect is achieved is still not precisely understood. It appears to be due to an effect on small structures within cells that are called 'mitochondria'.

Seven minutes has been suggested as the optimum duration for laser therapy. Treatment in acute cases should be daily, but for less acute cases treatment every three days is adequate. Laboratory tests suggest that the actual wavelength of the light emitted is not crucial in itself, although it may affect the penetrating power of the laser.

MAGNETIC FIELD THERAPY

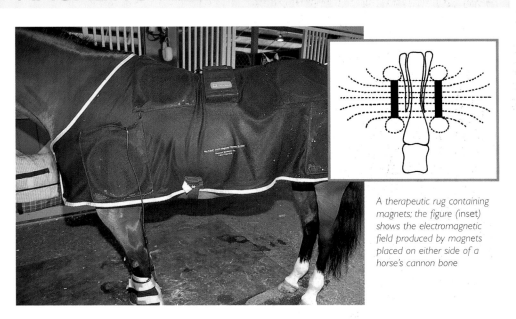

A therapeutic rug containing magnets; the figure (inset) shows the electromagnetic field produced by magnets placed on either side of a horse's cannon bone

MAGNETIC FIELD THERAPY may use fixed fields from static magnets, or it may use pulsing magnetic fields produced electrically. Scientific research on magnetic therapy has largely concentrated on the value of pulsing magnetic fields in stimulating or speeding up the healing of bone fractures. The theory is that they increase the activity of cells involved in the healing process.

It can certainly be said that neither form of magnetic therapy will cause any harm, and many horse owners have reported that chronic problems such as chronically swollen sprained tendons or arthritic joints have improved with magnetic field therapy.

HEMIPLEGIA

HEMIPLEGIA means half paralysed – meaning that half the anatomical structure is paralysed, rather than the whole structure being partially paralysed. In the horse the structure to which the term is most commonly applied is the larynx, or voice box. Laryngeal hemiplegia means that the muscles that control the vocal cords on one side of the larynx are paralysed. Hemiplegia occurs when the nerve supplying a group of muscles is damaged, rather than as a result of damage to the muscle itself – though with time, of course, the muscle becomes weak anyway, because of lack of activity.

ANAEMIA

ANAEMIA is a reduced amount of haemoglobin in the blood. As haemoglobin is the substance that carries oxygen around the body, a horse with anaemia has a greatly reduced metabolism; this means there will be a problem anywhere that oxygen is needed.

Anaemia can occur when there is a straight shortage of the red blood cells that contain the haemoglobin, perhaps because blood has been lost as a result of haemorrhage; or it can occur when the red blood cells have been destroyed in the body in some way. Anaemia can also occur when there are normal numbers of red blood cells, but each cell contains less haemoglobin than normal. This may occur if there is a shortage of iron, because iron is one of the essential components of haemoglobin.

We certainly cannot diagnose anaemia by looking at the pink membranes around a horse's mouth or eyes: by the time they are sufficiently pale for it to be obvious to the human eye, it would be a very serious anaemia indeed. However, a blood sample will show low haemoglobin levels, and that makes the diagnosis. There may or may not be low numbers of red blood cells present, and this may or may not reduce the packed cell volume, or PCV.

It takes a horse approximately a month to make a red blood cell from start to finish. It will therefore take a similar time to reverse anaemia. When the horse does make new red blood cells in such circumstances, the cells may at first be larger than normal. It is an encouraging sign in anaemia to find that such so-called macrocytic cells are already present.

There is a considerable amount of folk law about treating anaemia. Vitamin B_{12}

Grazing should prevent iron deficiency that could lead to anaemia

supplements have been given almost magical properties in this respect, whereas in real life it is impossible to produce a vitamin B_{12} deficiency in the normal horse, and so no supplements are needed. Only in horses undergoing extreme exercise will B_{12} affect the red blood cell production. Iron deficiency is also unlikely to limit red blood cell production in grazing horses because they take in small amounts of soil containing iron with the grass that they eat. There is a small chance of deficiency in horses that are stabled continuously. The only substance that has been shown to increase red blood cell production when fed to the normal horse is folic acid.

HERNIA

THE ABDOMINAL CAVITY is lined with a transparent membrane called the 'peritoneum', and is surrounded by a muscular wall. A hernia occurs when there is a gap in that wall that allows a pouch of peritoneum to push through, taking

Foal with umbilical hernia

with it part, or all, of an abdominal structure. The gap in the body wall is called the hernia ring. We recognise hernias as soft swellings under the skin that have definite structures within them, rather than liquid. They are not warm to the touch and are usually painless.

Perhaps the commonest hernia is the umbilical hernia seen in foals from birth. It is situated around the navel and represents a failure of the wall of the abdomen to be completely sealed as the foal was developing in its mother's womb. Hernias do not continue increasing in size with time. Nor do they decrease in size, although because the hernia ring does not grow like the rest of the body it may appear as if it is getting smaller in relation to the rest of the body. Hernias can cause problems when a loop of bowel from within the abdomen passes through the hernial ring but cannot pull back. Pressure on the loop of bowel can then cause the loop to start to die or to become strangulated. In other cases the ring may be large enough for bowel to pass in and out from time to time, giving a hernia that varies slightly in size.

FOREIGN BODY

IN MEDICAL TERMS A FOREIGN BODY is something that comes from outside the animal concerned, but which has in some way become fixed in the animal. Examples might include a grass seed up a horse's nose or a sliver of wood that has penetrated underneath the skin. Sometimes the foreign body also carries bacteria with it, resulting in a localised infection around it. Even if this does not happen, there will be a reaction around the foreign body just because the horse's body does not recognise it. These reactions will continue until the foreign body is removed. As a result there might be pus discharging from the place where the sliver of wood entered, and with antibiotics this may stop discharging for a time; however, it will return at a later date because the focus of the infection is still present.

HEART MURMUR

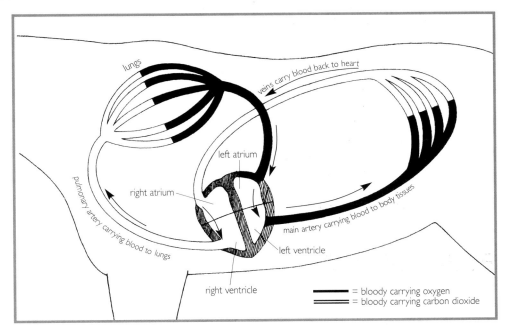

lungs

veins carry blood back to heart

left atrium

right atrium

pulmonary artery carrying blood to lungs

main artery carrying blood to body tissues

left ventricle

right ventricle

= bloody carrying oxygen
= bloody carrying carbon dioxide

Heart murmurs reflect turbulence as blood enters or leaves the four chambers of the heart

A HEART MURMUR is an additional heart sound. It may be between the normal lub-dub sounds, in which case it is said to be a diastolic murmur, or it may be associated with the lub and the dub, in which case it is said to be a systolic murmur. Murmurs are also graded according to their volume. So a grade 1 murmur is faint even when listening carefully to the heart with a stethoscope, but a grade 1V murmur might be heard even before the stethoscope actually comes into contact with the skin.

A murmur is the noise caused by turbulence in the blood flow. This might be caused by nothing more sinister than a change in the viscosity of the blood, affecting how it passes through the heart valves. Horses with anaemia may have a quite marked heart murmur, but this disappears when the number of red blood cells, and so the viscosity, returns to normal. Murmurs can also be caused by physical abnormalities of one of the valves, interfering with normal blood flow. By listening carefully we can locate the position where the murmur is at its loudest, and so make an informed guess as to which valve or other structure is most likely to be involved.

It has traditionally been assumed that a heart murmur that becomes more marked with exercise is more significant clinically than one which is less marked after strenuous exercise; but this is not always the case.

HEART ARRHYTHMIAS

ABNORMAL HEART RHYTHMS represent an abnormal sequence of the heart chambers filling and emptying, in conjunction with an abnormal sequence of heart valve opening and closing. The heart is normally controlled by electrical impulses that spread along precise pathways within the heart, activating contraction of muscles and opening or closing of valves as they do so. The simplest form of arrhythmia to understand is a heart block, where the impulse either comes to a complete stop or is delayed as it tries to pass along a damaged section of pathway. The part of the heart cycle that comes after this point will either be delayed, or will just not happen at all. So we might hear lub-dub, lub-dub, lub——-dub, or even lub-dub, lub-dub, lub———, lub-dub.

Clinically arrhythmias tend to be more significant than heart murmurs.

ESTIMATING WEIGHT

MOST DRUGS rely on the correct dose being given for maximum effect, and that dose is weight dependent. It is extremely difficult to guess a horse's weight visually, even for an experienced horse owner or vet. It is, however, possible to make a very accurate (within 10 per cent) estimate from two simple measurements: these are the horse's girth just behind the elbow, and the length of the body from the point of the elbow to the tuber ischii (the bony prominence just to the side of the tail area). If you make the measurement in inches, the formula is:

$$\text{Weight in pounds} = \frac{\text{girth x length x length}}{300}$$

If you make the measurements in centimetres, the formula is:

$$\text{Weight in kilograms} = \frac{\text{girth x length x length}}{12,000}$$

MALIGNANT/BENIGN TUMOUR

A BENIGN TUMOUR is one that does not have a tendency to form secondary tumours in other parts of the body. In contrast, a malignant tumour is likely to form other tumours elsewhere.

It is possible to have a benign tumour which, because of its sheer size or its anatomical position, causes serious clinical symptoms. It is also possible to have a small malignant tumour that at this time is causing no obvious symptoms at all. Nevertheless, a malignant tumour is always a time bomb with an unknown fuse, and even if it is removed surgically, further tumours are likely to occur later.

ANAESTHESIA

LITERALLY ANAESTHESIA MEANS without sensation. It is not just the removal of pain – a horse may not feel pain from a wound, but if you touch it, the horse will still react by kicking. Some sedatives may make the horse appear very sleepy, but it can still kick accurately when you touch the sore area.

Local anaesthesia removes sensation from just a localised area. It is achieved either by blocking a major nerve that supplies the area, or by injecting a number of small amounts of local anaesthetic solution all around the area so that any small nerve endings entering it will come into contact with the local anaesthetic solution.

General anaesthesia removes all sensation: the horse is to all intents and purposes unconscious, and it will not remember anything when it recovers. It must be understood that there is always a risk associated with general anaesthesia in the horse, which is why vets require the owner to sign a consent form beforehand to say that they accept the risk. Although equine anaesthesia has

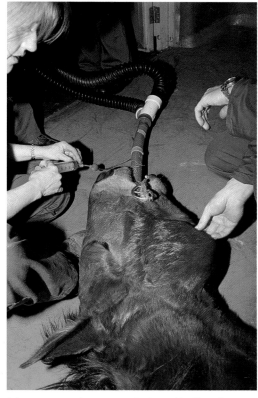

A horse connected to an anaesthetic machine. The tube goes into the horse's trachea

improved in leaps and bounds over recent years, the risk of death associated with it is still about six times that for a human being. One of the reasons for this is the sheer weight and size of the horse, because when it collapses to the ground it can all too easily injure itself. A full stomach or intestine is vulnerable at this stage, which is why a horse is ideally starved for 12–24 hours before it is given a general anaesthetic. The same risk is present when the horse recovers from the anaesthetic. The sheer weight of the horse also means that if breathing is depressed by the chemical effect of the anaesthetic, then the horse may not be able to fully expand the lungs against the weight of the chest.

The other major problem is that the muscles trapped between the horse's body and the ground lose their blood supply because the small blood vessels are squashed shut – and obviously the longer the anaesthetic lasts, the greater the risk of this happening. When the horse later tries to stand, the muscle is for all practical purposes paralysed, and cannot take any weight. Padding the floor of the anaesthetic room or the surface of the operating table is vitally important if this is to be avoided.

General anaesthesia has four stages. First the horse is sedated: this relaxes it, and makes the second stage, the induction, much smoother and safer. Induction has to be rapid and safe, and vets generally use a drug such as ketamine or thiopentone injected intravenously. Stage three is the maintenance of anaesthesia beyond the initial 10–12min. Usually this is achieved by using a gas formed by passing oxygen over a liquid anaesthetic agent such as halothane or isoflurane, forming a vapour. A large tube is passed through the horse's mouth and down into its trachea, or windpipe, to make sure that it breathes in a set percentage of the anaesthetic gas. The volume of air breathed in and out by the horse is very large, making the components of an equine anaesthetic machine similarly large. Sometimes anaesthesia is maintained by further injections of the intravenous induction agent. Finally comes recovery, with the horse getting safely to its feet.

ACUPUNCTURE

ACUPUNCTURE is an old Chinese therapy. As traditionally taught, it consists of using fine needles inserted through the skin to stimulate specific acupuncture points that lie along the energy streams Ying and Yang in the body. Acupuncture is not just concerned with the relief of pain: it also claims to restore normal function and well-being to the body. The acupuncture points can actually be stimulated in a variety of ways, including using just a beam of laser light. We now know that the points coincide with the sympathetic and parasympathetic nervous systems, the systems that control vital functions such as the heart rate, sweating and so on.

Not everyone can bring themselves to abandon modern science and accept so-called alternative medicine methods such as acupuncture. However, we do not have to do so. We can accept the technique and its effect without accepting the traditional explanation of how it works. In many countries it is legal for someone without any recognised training to carry out acupuncture therapy, only the actual act of diagnosis being restricted to qualified vets. As a result, acupuncture may fail to be effective because of poor technique on behalf of the operator, rather than from any other cause.

PHOTOSENSITIVITY

THE SKIN'S PROTECTION against the sun's ultra violet rays comes from a black pigment called melanin, which is inside the skin cells. When the natural protective screen is disrupted, severe burning of the skin occurs. The skin blisters, becomes inflamed and large areas of surface skin cells die.
Such photosensitivity, or hypersensitivity to sunlight, can be triggered off by eating poisonous plants eg St John's Wort, and can also arise from liver damage.
Unpigmented skin, where any hairs are white, is extremely susceptible.

ANIMALINTEX POULTICE

THIS POULTICE uses warm, but not boiling, water to activate the powder impregnated into a multi-layered gauze dressing. But poultices can damage wound edges, so a poulticed wound will take longer to heal than a non-poulticed one. You have to decide whether drawing pus out of a wound will compensate for this.

All poultices have a limited period of activity. An Animalintex dressing should be replaced twice daily.

In an emergency Animalintex can also be used as a dry absorbent pad rather than as a poultice.

1 Soak a piece of dressing, cut to roughly the size of the sole, in clean warm water. Do not use boiling water as this will be far too hot to apply to the horse's foot. Allow the dressing to drain. Avoid contamination by touching it as little as possible.

2 Lift the affected hoof and place the wet dressing on the sole, folding the edges over the hoof and making sure it is firmly in place. Use a self-adhesive bandage to secure it. First wrap the bandage around the outside of the hoof a few times, allowing the projecting edge to curl over the bottom of the foot.

3 Bring the bandage across the sole in one direction and go once round the foot again. Then go across the sole the other way.

4 Make as many more crosses over the sole as are necessary to ensure it is fully covered, then press the bandage to itself to stick it down. Cut off any excess bandage and smooth the edges to ensure there are no loose ends to catch or cause the dressing to be pulled off.

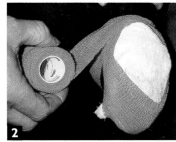

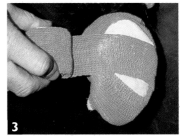

BANDAGING THE HOOF

IT IS PARTICULARLY DIFFICULT to hold dressings in place on the hoof without the bandage becoming loose as soon as the horse moves around. The bandage can become urine soaked, dirty and worn through unless an outer waterproof layer, such as a thick polythene bag, is applied over it. A Shoof or Equiboot can be used to hold dressings or a poultice in place. Use a co-adhesive bandage, so that each turn of the bandage sticks to the one it partly covers, but not to the skin.

ROBERT JONES BANDAGE

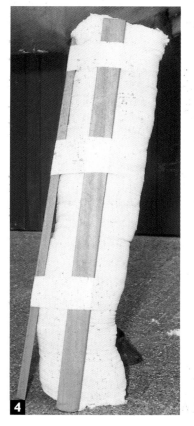

EVERY HORSE OWNER should know how to apply a Robert Jones bandage; he/she should also have the necessary materials, available both at the stable and in any horse transport they use. For any acute leg injury, whether it involves the tendons, the ligaments of a joint or the bones, it can never be wrong to apply pressure and to immobilise the leg, which is just what the Robert Jones bandage does, until you can get proper veterinary help. A Robert Jones bandage consists of four or more layers of either cotton wool or gamgee, each one held tightly in place by either crepe or, better still, adhesive bandages.

1   An initial layer of gamgee is wrapped around the leg.
2   This is held in place by a firmly applied bandage.
3   Further layers of padding are built up, with four being the minimum.
4   If necessary a sturdy piece of wood, such as a broom handle or a piece of plastic guttering can be incorporated to provide complete rigidity.

To provide proper immobility the Robert Jones bandage should extend from the top of the leg right down to, and including, the foot. It requires considerable bandaging materials and so is expensive to apply, but even fractured bones can be stabilised enough in this way to prevent further damage occurring.

BANDAGING THE HOCK

THE HOCK is a very difficult joint to bandage, combining as it does an awkward wedge shape with considerable movement. Use an adhesive bandage, so that each turn of bandage sticks to the one it partly covers.

1   The first step is to anchor the bandage by a couple of turns above the hock. Then make a diagonal and anchor it below the joint

2   Then use a figure-of-eight pattern to include the whole joint, taking care not to put too much pressure over the point of the hock.

3   Repeat until most of the joint is covered, then finish with some horizontal turns below the hock. It may help to apply a separate stable bandage up the cannon to the bottom border of the hock bandage. This provides a ledge to prevent the hock bandage slipping down.

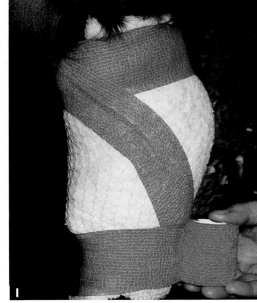

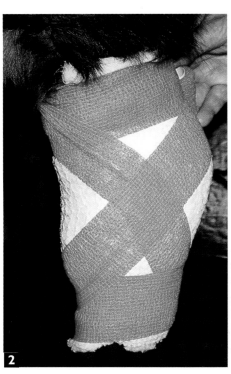

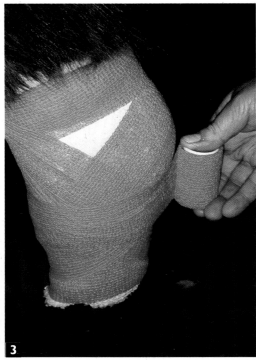

TWITCHING A HORSE

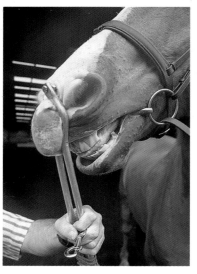

A TWITCH applies firm pressure to the horse's upper lip. This pressure appears to cause the release of endorphins, the body's natural morphine-like substances, into the bloodstream. The pressure may be applied by putting a loop of rope around the lip and twisting it until it is tight enough that even if the horse pulls away, it cannot pull free. The use of a twine or chain twitch is more likely to damage the lip.

A hinged and shaped smooth metal twitch does not mark the lip and appears to cause less resentment whilst producing greater restraint. It can also be fastened to the horse's headcollar rather than needing to be held by a handler.

Whatever the mechanism by which it works, there is no disputing the effect of a twitch. Even sedated horses are less likely to react adversely to stimuli if they are also twitched.

A hinged, metal twitch

FLEXION TESTS

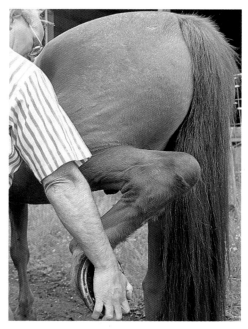

ALTHOUGH A HORSE BENDS ITS KNEE, stifle, hock and fetlock joints whenever it walks, even at the gallop it does not do so to their maximum extent. Bending these joints to their limit when there is a joint problem such as DJD will often make the horse lame if it is not already lame, or will make an existing lameness worse. Flexion tests do just that.

For the fore leg, the knee is bent to right angles and the fetlock joint is bent as far as it can go. One of the controversial aspects of flexion tests is that different vets put differing amounts of force on the fetlock joint. However, each vet uses the same degree of force each time they carry out the test, so that a particular vet is always comparing like with like. The joints are held flexed for a minimum of 30 seconds. Again, vets vary as regards the time they use, but each vet uses the same length of time each time they do the test. The leg is then

Flexion test of the hind leg. Care should be taken to avoid a hand injury should the horse kick out

released, and the horse immediately trotted off from the standing position. Any effect shows in the first half dozen strides, and may wear off again by the end of the short trot. When carrying out flexion tests on the hind legs, all three joints – the stifle, hock and fetlock – are flexed to their maximum.

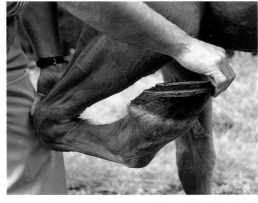

Flexion test of the foreleg

Not all vets are convinced as to the value of flexion tests, and they are not a compulsory part of the veterinary examination prior to purchase, although they are frequently performed during it. They are non-specific, in that they do not pinpoint either a particular condition or a particular joint; however, in my opinion they are a quick and cheap screening test. The results obtained by one vet cannot be directly compared with those obtained by another vet, but that does not usually matter in practice. There are a few horses that do show a degree of lameness after a flexion test every time it is performed, but never go properly lame otherwise. As long as a horse is not condemned solely on the grounds of a positive flexion test, this also does not affect the overall practical value of the test.

CLEANING A WOUND

ALTHOUGH MOST HORSE OWNERS appreciate the importance of cleaning a wound, very few know how to do so properly. The following procedure should be observed:

1   Wounds should be cleaned with boiled water that has cooled down, or with saline. Disinfectants should never be added, and antiseptics should only be used at very low concentrations: chlorhexidine is the safest.
2   If the skin surrounding the wound is very dirty, first protect the open wound itself with Intrasite Gel or similar, and then clean the surrounding area.
3   Next, clean the wound itself. You can do this by sponging gently from the centre of the wound outwards. Any gel you applied will wash away easily, taking a lot of the dirt with it. Never *hose* a wound with water, because this will wash any dirt deeper into it. The best way to wash a large wound is with water, but using a refillable hand spray (such as are sold by hairdressers and garden centres). Take time to get the wound clean.
4   Finally, again fill the wound itself with Intrasite Gel or similar. If possible cover with a non-adhesive dressing, and bandage this in place.

A wound treated in this way will not deteriorate further, and it will still be possible to suture such a wound 24–36 hours later, if appropriate. If suturing is not necessary – and I would suggest that a wound more than 2.5cm long should be stitched – the cleaning process should be repeated daily for four days, removing the old gel and replacing it each time. After four days the period between dressing changes can be lengthened.

ARTERY/VEIN

THE TERMS 'ARTERY' AND 'VEIN' are familiar enough, but not everyone understands the difference between them. Arteries pump blood away from the heart, and have muscular walls to help in doing so. Veins drain blood back to the heart quite passively. There are big veins and there are small arteries – size is nothing to do with it. Bleeding from an artery in a horse will always pulse, whether inches or feet away from the wound. Bleeding from a vein may pulse slightly, but only at the surface. Arterial blood is said to be brighter red in colour than venous blood, but you have to have experience to differentiate between them.

Because of the force of the blood pressure behind it, haemorrhage – or bleeding – from an artery is difficult to stop. Any clotting tends to get washed away before it can become properly established. Bleeding from anything other than one of the really major veins, on the other hand, can usually be stopped by firm pressure, which allows a clot to form and stabilise. This process can take up to 30 minutes.

As the arteries branch and become smaller and smaller they eventually become capillaries, which are the halfway stage between arteries and veins. It is in the capillaries that blood is moving slowly enough for oxygen and nutrition to diffuse out into the tissues, and for carbon dioxide and waste products to diffuse back in.

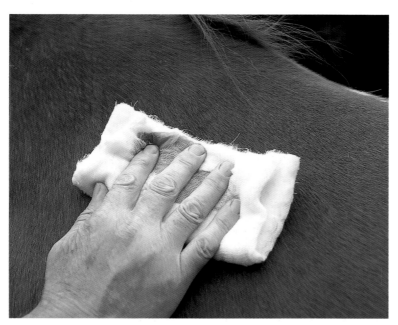

Applying firm pressure with a clean pad will help to slow or stop bleeding

PLASMA/SERUM

ALTHOUGH we sometimes treat these two words as being interchangeable, there is a significant difference between them. Plasma is blood minus the cells. Serum, on the other hand, is blood after clotting has taken place. So plasma occurs naturally in the body, passing in and out of the blood vessels, whereas serum only occurs in the body after haemorrhage. Plasma will clot because it contains a substance called fibrinogen; serum cannot clot, and always remains a fluid. However, serum does still contain antibodies, and can be used to transfer those antibodies to another horse that needs them.

BACTERIA/VIRUS

BACTERIA are small, single-celled organisms that have an independent life. Because they multiply by dividing into two, and can in ideal circumstances do this every 30 minutes, they are usually found in very large numbers. They cannot be seen with the naked eye, but can be seen under an ordinary light microscope.

Not all bacteria are harmful. The large colon of the horse contains large numbers of bacteria whose sole role is to digest the fructans from plant material that otherwise the horse would not be able to digest. Bacteria can be killed by a group of compounds called antibiotics.

Viruses are much smaller single-celled organisms. They cannot be seen under the light microscope, and it was not until the invention of the electron microscope that we could see that they really did exist. Viruses multiply by entering a cell in the host animal and adapting its nucleus to make new virus particles.

Viruses are not killed by antibiotics, being protected from them by having their replication take place safely inside a host cell. The down side of this is that viruses cannot survive away from their host for any significant length of time. They may not necessarily cause disease in every animal they infect, but they are certainly not advantageous to their host.

RESPIRATORY RATE

THE NORMAL RESPIRATORY rate in the resting healthy horse is 8–16 breaths per minute. Any rate of 20 or more per minute is significant. Large horses tend to have a slightly lower respiratory rate than small ponies.

The respiratory rate at the canter and gallop is linked to the stride rate, as the horse must breathe out when its lead leg hits the ground. There is also a link between the respiratory rate and the heart rate, with the ratio being approximately 1:3 respectively. When there are serious lung problems such as pneumonia, the respiratory rate increases and the ratio can reach 1:1.

LYMPH GLANDS

TISSUE FLUID drains back into the general circulation via thin-walled tubes called lymphatics. Scattered throughout this drainage system are numerous lymph glands, whose role is to filter out any infectious organisms and trap them whilst the immune system deals with them. The glands become swollen when they do trap infection or are stimulated by the immune system. As an example, the numerous glands around the throat region become swollen during a respiratory infection that gains entry via the membranes in the nose and pharynx. Sometimes abscesses form in the glands, which then become hot and painful. This commonly occurs in strangles, and almost all the symptoms of strangles are associated with the abscesses that form in the lymph glands.

Although the glands can swell up quite quickly, they take much longer to return to normal size after the infection has been overcome, and sometimes they remain swollen for months or years.

NERVOUS SYSTEMS (sympathetic/parasymphetic)

THESE ARE TWO DISTINCT but complementary systems of nerves that control such automatic processes as the beating of the heart or the secretions from various glands.

The parasympathetic system has sections involving some cranial nerves, the vagus nerve, and some of the sacral nerves near the pelvis. The sympathetic system has fibres in the spinal nerves of the neck and in the lumbar region just behind the ribs. The systems oppose each other. So the parasympathetic system contracts the pupil, but the sympathetic system dilates it. The sympathetic system causes secretion of sweat, but the parasympathetic system does not. On the other hand, the sympathetic system causes dilation of the bronchioles in the lungs, but the parasympathetic system causes their constriction.

ABORTION

ANY BIRTH earlier than the normal term is considered an abortion. Normality for the horse is fairly flexible, which means to say that if the 'normal' length of pregnancy, or gestation, for a mare is 340 days, then anything within 30 days either side of that can be a normal full-term birth.

There is a tendency to use the term 'abortion' for when the pregnancy ends in a dead foal, but to call a weak foal that lives even for a short time a premature foal. An aborted foal and a stillborn foal can mean the same thing. Mares that have a longer-than-normal oestrus cycle after breeding may have initially conceived, but subsequently aborted the embryo. So the term 'abortion' does not necessarily mean that there will be a visible outward symptom of the end of the pregnancy, nor that a recognisable foetus will be expelled from the mare's uterus.

When a number of mares in the same area abort as a result of the same cause, it is often referred to as an abortion storm.

ATAXIA

ATAXIA is a weakness of the muscles controlling the horse's ability to stand or move around. As a result of ataxia the horse may sway from side to side, or it may fall right over. Sometimes only the hind legs are affected, the rest of the body being apparently normal. In other cases both front and hind legs are affected.

The muscle weakness is usually the result of a lack of normal stimulation or control from the nerves that supply that muscle. Sometimes it can be difficult to appreciate slight ataxia. However, the standard test is to walk alongside a horse's hind legs as it walks or trots in hand, holding on to the tail. In the normal horse if you attempt to pull the hindquarters towards you, the muscles will compensate and keep it on course. However, you can pull an ataxic horse off course in this way quite readily.

Testing for ataxia by pulling the horse's quarters across while it is trotting

JAUNDICE

Hold the eye open with finger and thumb to assess the surrounding membrane

JAUNDICE is a yellow coloration of the otherwise pink membranes of the eyes and mouth. It is also referred to as 'icterus'. The eye membranes are the best ones by which to assess jaundice, because the horse's tongue can be quite yellowish in a healthy horse anyway. The colour is due to the build-up of pigment in the blood that should have been removed by the liver. Although not common in the horse, jaundice does occur in liver disease, although the degree of yellow coloration does not provide a guide to the degree of liver damage.

FUNGI

FUNGI differ from bacteria in that the cells are linked together into groups or filaments that in turn may form structures visible to the naked eye. Nonetheless, each individual cell is relatively non-specialised and can survive on its own without the need for common services such as a blood supply. Fungi obtain their nutrients from the host organism, or from organic material on which they live. Fungal diseases tend not to be very host specific, so ringworm can infect both the horse and its rider. Aspergillosis, for example, can cause abortion if it invades the reproductive system, but pneumonia if it invades the respiratory system.

HOT & COLD FOMENTATIONS

A FOMENTATION is the application of either a hot or a cold object to the skin in order to heat up or cool down a localised area.

Hot fomentations can be as simple as a cloth that has been soaked in warm water, squeezed out and folded into a pad before being placed on the skin. Care must be taken that the fomentation is not too hot, so test it against the inside of your wrist first to check that it is bearable. Hot poultices are also fomentations, although they may in addition involve a chemical action as well as heat. The main aim of a hot fomentation is to increase the local blood supply to the area. Because this in turn results in more blood cells being present, it speeds up the body's ability to deal with local infection. It also improves the removal of waste products from the area, including some of the substances produced during inflammation that otherwise make the area so painful.

Cold fomentations most commonly use ice in various forms to cool a localised area. Never put ice directly onto a horse's skin, as this may produce similar damage to a burn; always have at least one layer of padding or bandage between the ice and the skin. Alternatives to ice include packets of frozen food (frozen peas mould well to the shape of the body) or just cold water. Cold fomentations warm up surprisingly rapidly at the point of contact with the skin and need to be refreshed or replaced quite frequently. It has been claimed that hosing with cold water is more effective at cooling the area than an ice pack because of the difficulties in ensuring complete contact between the ice and the irregular outline of the horse's leg, and because the cold water is constantly changed. Cold fomentations cause constriction of the small blood vessels and so reduce the blood supply to the area. They are used during the early stages of inflammation to prevent the blood supply bringing the substances that cause the inflammatory reactions of heat, pain and swelling into the area.

The efficacy of both hot and cold fomentations is increased by firm, gentle pressure to ensure even contact all over the area, and by regular replacement at the correct temperature.

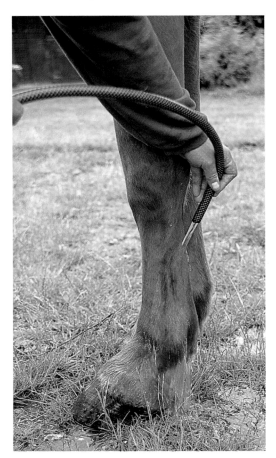

Hosing with cold water is the simplest way to apply a fomentation to the leg

A specially-made boot that can apply a flow of water to a strained or injured leg via a hose attachment

HAEMORRHAGE

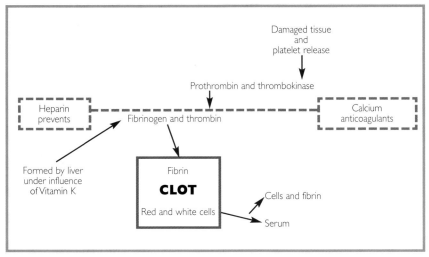

Damaged tissue
and
platelet release

Prothrombin and thrombokinase

Heparin
prevents

Fibrinogen and thrombin

Calcium
anticoagulants

Formed by liver
under influence
of Vitamin K

Fibrin

CLOT

Red and white cells

Cells and fibrin

Serum

The clotting mechanism: platelets are released at the site of a wound, starting a chain reaction which leads to the production of fibrin, which traps blood cells to make a clot

HAEMORRHAGE, or bleeding, from damaged tissues is never desirable, so forget the old wives' tale about it being good because it washes dirt out of a wound. The better the blood supply to an area, the more readily it will bleed, although it is also often true that in such areas the blood vessels are more likely to be relatively small. The blood has a built-in clotting mechanism of course, that relies on the presence of oxygen to trigger off the process. All the necessary building blocks to form a clot are always to hand in the blood, but clotting does not usually occur in undamaged blood vessels. The most crucial substance is a protein called fibrin that forms a network of fibres bridging the gaps in the blood vessel wall as the framework for a clot.

The secret to stopping bleeding is to stop blood flow through the break in the blood vessel wall for long enough for a network of fibrin fibres to become firmly attached right across the break. It might be that firm pressure on the wound, using a pad held or bandaged in place, will be sufficient to allow clotting to take place – though take care when lifting the pad to check if this is the case, because you don't want to pull the clot away from the blood vessel with the pad. With large breaks in the wall of a vein, or even small breaks in arteries where the blood pressure seeking to escape is higher, pressure alone might not be enough to stop bleeding and the vet may need to put a clamp across the ruptured blood vessel just before the break. If the pressure in that blood vessel is not too great, when the clamp is removed the opposing sides of the blood vessel wall will remain stuck to each other and no blood will escape. Failing this, the vet will have to tie a piece of suture material (nowadays usually an absorbable synthetic thread) around the blood vessel.

IDEOPATHIC DISEASE

AN IDEOPATHIC DISEASE is one that arises without the need for any stimulation from elsewhere in the body, or any cause from outside the horse's body. In many cases an ideopathic disease therefore comes to mean one whose cause is unknown.

ANOXIA

ANOXIA means that there is an absence of oxygen. It results from interruption of the blood supply that normally brings oxygen to that area. As all living tissues ultimately rely on oxygen for their metabolism, anoxia results in the short term in the tissue ceasing to function, and in the long term in its death.

HORMONE

A HORMONE is a substance that controls a body function some distance from where the hormone itself is manufactured or released; for example, follicle-stimulating hormone (FSH) that is secreted by the pituitary gland in the head, causes the follicle(s) to grow in the ovary. Often there are specific glands that produce one or more hormones, for example the thyroid gland and the pituitary gland. These glands themselves may be controlled by nerve impulses from the sympathetic/parasympathetic systems, or even by other hormones.

Hormone levels in the blood can be measured in the laboratory, and a raised level may be just as dangerous as a deficiency. So the thyroid gland can cause symptoms of disease from both hyper activity (too much hormone being produced) and hypo activity (too little hormone being produced).

BOWEL FLORA

THE HORSE RELIES on harmless bacteria living in its caecum and large intestine to digest plant material such as cellulose that other mammals, such as ourselves, cannot. The bacteria are present in very large numbers, consisting of numerous different bacterial families. A natural balance develops supporting a blend of bacterial types that most effectively deals with the diet that the horse is receiving at that time. Sudden changes in diet result in undigested material passing through the gut, and the large numbers of bacteria that are now 'unemployed' can cause problems such as diarrhoea.

MEAN CORPUSCULAR VOLUME (MCV)

RED BLOOD CELLS are very small in size. It is not practical to measure the size of individual cells, so instead the total volume of the red cells in each millilitre of blood is measured, and this is divided by the number of cells in the same volume to give the mean corpuscular volume. The significance of the MCV lies in distinguishing between different types of anaemia. Macrocytic anaemia has cells with a larger-than-normal MCV, and usually indicates that there are new, immature red blood cells being released into the bloodstream. Microcytic anaemia means that the cells have a low MCV, and indicates that there is a shortage of the raw materials needed to manufacture red blood cells, for example as in iron deficiency.

NEUTROPHILS

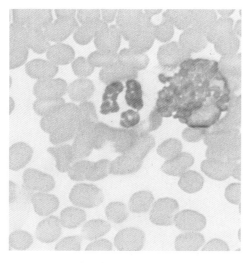

White blood cells under the microscope

WHITE BLOOD CELLS, or neutrophils, are divided into four types, depending on the structure of their nucleus and the way it responds to stains applied when we look at blood smears under a microscope. Conveniently, each of the four groups has a different function as well.

Leucocytes are the cells that kill bacteria: so if a horse has a major bacterial infection, its blood will usually have a leucocytosis (high numbers of leucocytes). Monocytes and lymphocytes are involved in the body's antibody production and in its response to viruses. Lymphopaenia (low numbers of lymphocytes) occurs during viral infections. Eosinophils are concerned with allergic-type reactions, which may include the horse's response to the presence of parasites, but does not necessarily do so.

ROARING/OTHER RESPIRATORY SOUNDS

THE TERM 'ROARING' is used to describe a loud abnormal sound made as the horse breathes in during exercise. It is a rough sound caused by air turbulence in the larynx, or voicebox. Roaring must not be confused with the loud sound made when a normal horse breathes out during exercise. This sound always coincides with the horse's leading leg hitting the ground, and is more like a grunt.

SEDATIVES

IT IS IMPORTANT to remember that sedatives make the horse sleepy. They do not necessarily make it less responsive to stimuli, nor do they make it less able to control its muscles if it wishes to do so. Thus a sedated horse is perfectly capable of kicking out violently and accurately in response to someone touching its leg or a wound. It has been said that sedatives are most effective in quiet horses that are not stimulated in any way – which is, of course, the exact opposite of the situation when we most commonly seek to use them.

Acetylpromazine is a sedative that is active when given by mouth as well as by injection, and so is often supplied to horse owners for use when clipping an excitable horse, for example. Unfortunately it is a poor sedative, and giving increasing dosages may make it less effective rather than more. Romifidine and medetomidine are more recent sedatives that, when given by injection, are very effective in the horse. Indeed their use has revolutionised veterinary practice by enabling procedures to be safely carried out in the stable environment on a standing horse, rather than requiring general anaesthesia.

When it is desirable to reduce a horse's response to stimuli such as touching, a dose of butorphanol should be given approximately two minutes after the romfidine or medetomidine. This will usually enable mildly painful procedures to be carried out without any further precautions.

PROSTAGLANDINS

PROSTAGLANDINS are very powerful hormones that are involved in a number of functions. Therapeutically we use prostaglandins to cause the corpus luteum in a mare's ovary to be 'dissolved'. This structure prevents a mare coming into season, so its removal usually results in a heat period within 48 hours. Giving prostaglandins to a pregnant mare will cause an abortion, because in the early stages of pregnancy the corpus luteum maintains pregnancy, and in the later stages the hormone causes contractions of the uterine muscles which will push out the foetus.

CARBOHYDRATES

CARBOHYDRATES are organic compounds that contain just carbon, hydrogen and oxygen. Glucose is one of the simplest carbohydrates and is the basic fuel for energy production in the horse. Glucose is stored in the muscles in a chain formulation called glycogen. One of the main functions of digestion is to break down more complex carbohydrates such as starches and fructans to glucose, which can then be readily available as fuel for energy production.

SCAR TISSUE

When a wound heals, a significant amount of the new tissue is fibres of a protein called collagen. These are relatively inert and have very little elasticity. The scar tissue as a whole therefore has these same properties. Over a period of 3-6 weeks some of the other components of the new tissue contract, making the wound and its scar tissue smaller in size, but the scar tissue remaining is even less active. Scar tissue often does not have fair follicles an so remains bald.

CYSTS

A cyst is a hollow cavity in the body of another structure. The cavity may be filled with a secretion of some kind, especially when the cyst forms inside a gland. Cysts vary greatly in their size, but are basically benign structures that cause no harm other than perhaps making a structure such as a small skin gland significantly larger in size.

CELLULITIS

Cellulitis is an inflammation of the subcutaneous structures between the skin and the underlying tissue. Usually the inflammation is associated with infection. It is characterised by swelling and oedema of the area, which will feel warm to the touch. It is usually secondary to another problems such as a skin wound. Any infection involved will require antibiotics given by injection or orally to stop its spread.

SEPTICAEMIA

When bacteria are circulating in large numbers around the whole body in the blood stream the horse is said to have a general septicaemia. The symptoms will vary greatly depending on the particular bacteria involved, but the horse will usually have a raised temperature and be off colour. The circulating bacteria tend to multiply rapidly and have the potential to localise in any of the vital organs, so septicaemia is a very serious condition.

USEFUL ADDRESSES

UNITED KINGDOM
ADAS
Woodthorne, Wergs Road,
Wolverhampton WV6 8TQ

Animal Health Trust
Lanwades Park, Kentford, Newmarket,
Suffolk IP29 5UU

**Association of Chartered
Physiotherapists in Animal Therapy**
Morland House, Salters Lane, Winchester,
Hampshire SO22 5JP

British Equestrian Trade Association
East Wing, Stockeld Park, Wetherby,
West Yorkshire LS22 4AW

British Equine Veterinary Association
5 Finlay Street, London SW6 6HE

British Horse Society
Stoneleigh Deer Park, Kenilworth,
Warwickshire CV8 2XZ

British Veterinary Association
7 Mansfield Street, London W1M 0AT

The Donkey Sanctuary
Slade House Farm, Salcombe Regis, Sidmouth,
Devon EX10 0NU

Farriers Registration Council
Sefton House, Adam Court, Newark Road,
Peterborough, Lincolnshire PE1 5PP

National Equine Welfare Council
Stanton, 10 Wales Street, Kings Sutton, Banbury,
Oxfordshire OX17 3RR

National Foaling Bank
Meretown Stud, Meretown, Newport,
Shropshire TF10 8BX

The National Stud
Newmarket, Suffolk CB8 0XE

Royal College of Veterinary Surgeons
Belgravia House, 62-64 Horseferry Road,
London SW1P 2AF

Society of Master Saddlers
Kettles Farm, Mickfield, Stowmarket,
Suffolk IP14 6BY

NORTH AMERICA
American Farrier's Association
4059 Iron Works Pkwy. Suite 1, Lexington,
KY 40511, USA

**American Medical Equestrian
Association**
PO Box 130848, Birmingham,
AL 35213-0848, USA

American Veterinary Medical Association
1931 North Meacham Road, Suite 100,
Schaumburg, IL 60173, USA

Canadian Veterinary Medical Association
339 Booth Street, Ottawa, Ontario K1R 7K1,
Canada

**Saddle, Harness and Allied Trades
Association**
1101-A Broad Street, Oriental, NC 28571, USA

AUSTRALIA & NEW ZEALAND
Australian Veterinary Association
PO Box 371, Artarmon, NSW 1570, Australia

New Zealand Veterinary Association
PO Box 11-212, Manners Street, Wellington,
New Zealand

INDEX

Page numbers in **bold** type refer to main entries, which will generally include illustrations. *Italic* page numbers refer to picture captions.

ACKNOWLEDGMENTS

Photographs supplied by:
Matthew Roberts/© David & Charles p2
Kit Houghton: pp 10(top), 12, 20(btm), 21, 22, 28(left), 30,
  38(btm), 40, 42(top), 46(top), 50, 52(top), 54, 56, 58. 60,
  118, 121(top), 143(top), 163(left), 164, 165, 169
Colin Vogel: pp 16, 25(top), 26, 52(btm), 64, 65, 66, 67,
  68, 70, 71, 72, 73, 74, 76, 77, 78, 80, 81, 82, 83, 84, 85, 87, 90,
  93, 94, 96, 97, 98, 100, 101, 102, 103, 105, 107, 108, 110, 111,
  112, 113, 114, 115, 116, 117, 119, 120, 121(btm), 122, 123,
  124, 125, 127, 128, 129, 130, 131, 132, 133, 140, 145, 146,
  147, 148, 151, 152, 160, 162, 171, 172, 173, 181(rt), 184
Bob Langrish/© David & Charles pp24(btm)

Andrew Perkins/© David & Charles pp36, 42(btm), 46(btm),
  137, 138, 143(btm), 144, 150, 155, 157, 159, 174, 175, 176,
  179, 180, 181(left)
Colin Vogel would like to thank the Equine Department,
  Faculty of Veterinary Science, The University of Liverpool
  for their support and help in providing photographs.

Artwork by:
Maggie Raynor/© David & Charles p18, 44, 104, 149(btm)
Paul Bale/© David & Charles p35
Chartwell Illustrators/© David & Charles pp 41, 106, 109, 113,
Colin Vogel: pp 89, 92, 105, 161, 163(rt), 167